KNITTING
RUGS

KNITTING RUGS

39 traditional, contemporary, innovative designs

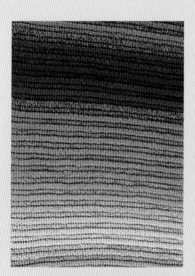

Nola Heidbreder and Linda Pietz

STACKPOLE
BOOKS

Published by
STACKPOLE BOOKS
5067 Ritter Road
Mechanicsburg, PA 17055
www.stackpolebooks.com

Printed in the United States of America

10 9 8 7 6 5 4 3 2 1

First edition

Cover design by Tessa J. Sweigert
Photography by Impact Xposures
Photographed at Crow's Foot Farm

Library of Congress Cataloging-in-Publication Data

Heidbreder, Nola.
  Knitting rugs / Nola Heidbreder and Linda Pietz.
    pages cm
  ISBN 978-0-8117-1251-4
  1. Rugs. 2. Knitting—Patterns. I. Pietz, Linda. II. Title.
  TT850.H45 2014
  746.7'3—dc23
                                                    2014014764

Soli Deo Gloriam

Many thanks to all of those who assisted and supported the writing of this book including Deb Smith, our family, the suppliers, Auburn Parks and Recreation, and the Knotty Knitters of Auburn and across the country.

Contents

Introduction

They say you should write the book that you would want on your bookshelf and that is precisely what we did. When we decided to write this book of patterns for knitted rugs, before one word was put to paper or one stitch knit, we brainstormed about what we, as knitters, would want in a book like this.

First, we wanted the rugs to be easy to make. Why create patterns that seem so impossible that no one would attempt to make them? Most of our rugs are easy enough for the confident beginner, but pleasurable enough to engage the experienced knitter. (Though lest you think all rugs in this book are for the novice knitter, there are a few that are a little more challenging!)

We also wanted rugs that were quick to knit. Considering all of the modern conveniences that are supposed to save us all this time, how is it that we are so busy? That being said, we all can find a few precious moments to indulge in a row or two of our latest project. We designed the rugs in this book to be relatively quick to knit, so that you can enjoy making them quickly and, even more exciting, enjoy using them.

In addition to easy and quick, we wanted the rugs to be fun to make! We just couldn't bring ourselves to create patterns that have you cast on, do a long stretch of mindless knitting, and then bind off. Among our collection of rugs are modular knits, mosaics, rugs made on a knitting spool, round rugs, rugs with holes, and even a rug with grass growing out of it. Knitting these rugs is anything but mindless!

Because of our love of history, we just had to include a few updates of historical rugs. And as we always like to say, our ancestors were the original recyclers, not throwing anything out, but cleverly reusing the limited resources they had. So along with the historical aspect of these rugs came the idea of repurposing materials such as wool work shirts and those T-shirts in our closets we all just hate to throw out.

As much as we love knitting, we also love all things fiber, such as traditional rug hooking, crocheting, quilting, appliqué, and weaving—to name just a few. We are betting that you are a fiber fanatic like we are and would enjoy adding some touches of those other disciplines into your rugs. So while many of the rugs in this book only use knitting techniques, there are a few that bring in other fiber arts in addition to knitting.

We know you will enjoy making these rugs as much as we enjoyed creating the patterns.

—Linda and Nola
The Rug Sisters

MODULAR RUGS

Module: An individual self-contained segment or unit.

L arge knitting projects can be tedious because of the large number of stitches. This is what makes modular knitting so wonderful—you can knit a large piece such as a rug a little bit at a time. The small pieces add variety, and completing each module gives you a sense of accomplishment. Another advantage to these rugs is that you can make them larger or smaller by adding or subtracting modules.

Rugs where each module is made separately, such as the Forest Floor rug and the Seaside Freeform Rug are great take-along projects. I always have what I call my "emergency knitting" with me wherever I go. You never know when you might have to sit waiting at the doctor's office or while your husband runs into the auto parts store. No problem—just pull out that leaf or kelp you're working on! The modules for these rugs are easy to carry with you, and let you make the most of unexpected downtime.

And trust me when I say don't forget your emergency knitting. I can tell you from experience: If I don't have it with me, things like the car breaking down happen, and there I am, waiting to be towed and all I can think of is how many modules I could have knitted.

Forest Floor

YARN

Cascade 220 (100% wool; 220 yd./200 m; 3.5 oz/100g), 2 skeins each of the following colors:

- **Color A:** Cafe (2411)
- **Color B:** Kansas (2437)
- **Color C:** Red Wine Heather (9489)
- **Color D:** Birch Heather (9564)
- **Color E:** Provence (2425)
- **Color F:** Fall Heather (9597)

NEEDLES
U.S. size 9 (5.5 mm) straight needles

NOTIONS
U.S. size I-9 (5.5 mm) crochet hook
Tapestry needle

GAUGE
4 sts = 1 in. (2.5 cm) in garter stitch

FINISHED MEASUREMENTS
36 by 24 in. (91 by 61 cm)

Each season has a beauty all its own, but there is just something about autumn. Is there anything better than a brilliant blue sky framed by splashes of orange, red, and yellow leaves? And when you stroll through a woodland glade on such a day, the forest floor is covered with a mosaic of leaves that have already fallen. This is the inspiration for this rug pattern.

Despite being botanically challenged, I have always had a fascination with leaf shapes. The basic shapes, captured in various shades of green and orange, lend themselves perfectly to a retro look. I've included a variation that makes great use of these shapes.

LEAF COLORS

Oak Leaf: Color A (veins in color B)
Narrow Leaf: Color B (veins in color A)
Maple Leaf: Color C (veins in color D)
Fan-Shaped Leaf: Color D (veins in color C)
Wavy Leaf: Color E (veins in color F)
Oval Leaf: Color F (veins in color E)

▦ PATTERN

Using the colors indicated above and two strands of yarn held together, knit at least 5 of each type of leaf.

OAK LEAF

CO 2 sts.
Row 1 (RS): Knit.
Row 2 (WS): Knit.
Row 3: Kfb twice. (4 sts)
Row 4: K3, kfb. (5 sts)
Row 5: Kfb, k3, kfb. (7 sts)
Row 6: Kfb, k5, kfb. (9 sts)
Row 7: Kfb, k7, kfb. (11 sts)
Row 8: Kfb, k9, kfb. (13 sts)
Row 9: Kfb, k to end. (14 sts)
Row 10: Kfb, k to last st, kfb. (16 sts)
Row 11: Knit.
Row 12: Ssk, k to last 2 sts, k2tog. (14 sts)
Row 13: Ssk, k to last 2 sts, k2tog. (12 sts)
Row 14: Using a knitted cast on, CO 2 sts. K to last st, kfb. (15 sts)
Row 15: Using a knitted cast on, CO 2 sts. K to last st, kfb. (18 sts)
Row 16: Using a knitted cast on, CO 2 sts. K to last st, kfb. (21 sts)
Row 17: Using a knitted cast on, CO 2 sts. K to last st, kfb. (24 sts)
Row 18: Using a knitted cast on, CO 2 sts. K to last st, kfb. (27 sts)
Row 19: Kfb, k to last st, kfb. (29 sts)
Row 20: Knit.
Row 21: BO 8 sts, k across the row to the last 2 sts, k2tog. (20 sts)
Row 22: BO 8 sts, k to end. (12 sts)
Row 23: Kfb, k to end. (13 sts)
Row 24: Kfb, k to end. (14 sts)
Row 25: Kfb, k to last st, kfb. (16 sts)
Row 26: Kfb, k to last st, kfb. (18 sts)
Row 27: Kfb, k to last st, kfb. (20 sts)
Row 28: Kfb, k to last st, kfb. (22 sts)
Row 29: Kfb, k to last st, kfb. (24 sts)
Row 30: K to last st, kfb. (25 sts)
Row 31: K to last 2 sts, k2tog. (24 sts)
Row 32: BO 7 sts, k to end. (17 sts)
Row 33: BO 7 sts, k to last st, kfb. (11 sts)
Row 34: K to last 2 sts, k2tog. (10 sts)
Row 35: K to last st, kfb. (11 sts)
Row 36: K to last st, kfb. (12 sts)
Row 37: Kfb, k to last st, kfb. (14 sts)
Row 38: K to last st, kfb. (15 sts)
Row 39: K to last 2 sts, k2tog. (14 sts)
Row 40: BO 3 sts, k to last 2 sts, k2tog. (10 sts)
Row 41: BO 3 sts, k to last 2 sts, k2tog. (6 sts)
Row 42: K to last 2 sts, k2tog. (5 sts)
Row 43: Knit.
Row 44: K to last 2 sts, k2tog. (4 sts)
Row 45: Knit.
Row 46: K2tog, ssk. (2 sts)
BO. Fasten off, leaving a long tail for sewing.

NARROW LEAF

CO 3 sts.
Row 1: Knit.
Row 2: Kfb, k to end. (4 sts)
Row 3: Kfb, k to end. (5 sts)
Row 4: Kfb, k to end. (6 sts)
Row 5: Kfb, k to end. (7 sts)
Row 6: Knit.
Row 7: K to last st, kfb. (8 sts)
Row 8: K to last st, kfb. (9 sts)
Row 9: Knit.
Row 10: Knit.
Row 11: Knit.
Row 12: Kfb, k to end. (10 sts)

Row 13: Kfb, k to end. (11 sts)
Rows 14–25: Knit.
Row 26: K to last 2 sts, k2tog. (10 sts)
Row 27: K to last 2 sts, k2tog. (9 sts)
Rows 28–33: Knit.
Row 34: Ssk, k to last 2 sts, k2tog. (7 sts)
Rows 35–38: Knit.
Row 39: K to last 2 sts, k2tog. (6 sts)
Row 40: K to last 2 sts, k2tog. (5 sts)
Row 41: Knit.
Row 42: Knit.
Row 43: K to last 2 sts, k2tog. (4 sts)
Row 44: Knit.
Row 45: Ssk, k to end. (3 sts)
Row 46: Ssk, k1. (2 sts)
Row 47: Knit.
Row 48: Sl 1, k1, psso.
Break yarn, leaving a long tail for sewing, and pull through
   remaining st.

MAPLE LEAF

CO 24 sts.
Row 1: Knit.
Row 2: CO 7 sts, k to last 2 sts, k2tog. (30 sts)
Row 3: Ssk, k to last 2 sts, k2tog. (28 sts)
Row 4: Ssk, k to last 2 sts, k2tog. (26 sts)
Row 5: Ssk, k to last 2 sts, k2tog. (24 sts)
Row 6: Ssk, k to last 2 sts, k2tog. (22 sts)
Row 7: K to last 2 sts, k2tog. (21 sts)
Row 8: K to last 2 sts, k2tog. (20 sts)
Row 9: Ssk, k to last 2 sts, k2tog. (18 sts)
Row 10: K to last 2 sts, k2tog. (17 sts)
Row 11: K to last st, kfb. (18 sts)
Row 12: Kfb, k to last st, kfb. (20 sts)
Row 13: Kfb, k to end. (21 sts)
Row 14: Kfb, k to last st, kfb. (23 sts)

Row 15: K to last st, kfb. (24 sts)
Row 16: Kfb, k to last st, kfb. (26 sts)
Row 17: Kfb, k to last st, kfb. (28 sts)
Row 18: Kfb, k to last st, kfb. (30 sts)
Row 19: Kfb, k to last st, kfb. (32 sts)
Row 20: Kfb, k to last st, kfb. (34 sts)
Row 21: Kfb, k to last st, kfb. (36 sts)
Row 22: BO 13 sts, k to last 2 sts, k2tog. (22 sts)
Row 23: BO 12 sts, k to last 2 sts, k2tog. (9 sts)
Row 24: K to last 2 sts, k2tog. (8 sts)
Row 25: Knit.
Row 26: Knit.
Row 27: Knit.
Row 28: K to last 2 sts, k2tog. (7 sts)
Row 29: K to last 2 sts, k2tog. (6 sts)
Row 30: Knit.
Row 31: Ssk, k to end. (5 sts)
Row 32: Knit.
Row 33: K to last 2 sts, k2tog. (4 sts)
Row 34: K to last 2 sts, k2tog. (3 sts)
Row 35: Knit.
Row 36: Knit.
Row 37: Knit.
Row 38: Ssk, k to end. (2 sts)
Row 39: Knit.
Row 40: Knit.
Row 41: Sl 1, k1, psso.
Break yarn, leaving a long tail for sewing, and pull through
   remaining st.

FAN-SHAPED LEAF

CO 2 sts.
Row 1: Knit.
Row 2: Kfb, k1. (3 sts)
Row 3: Kfb, k to last st, kfb. (5 sts)
Row 4: Kfb, k to last st, kfb. (7 sts)

Row 5: Using a knitted cast-on, CO 8 sts. K to last st, kfb. (16 sts)

Row 6: Using a knitted cast-on, CO 8 sts. K to last st, kfb. (25 sts)

Row 7: K to last st, kfb. (26 sts)

Row 8: Knit.

Row 9: K to last st, kfb. (27 sts)

Row 10: Knit.

Row 11: K to last 2 sts, k2tog. (26 sts)

Row 12: Knit.

Row 13: Ssk, k to last st. (25 sts)

Row 14: Knit.

Row 15: K to last 2 sts, k2tog. (24 sts)

Row 16: K to last 2 sts, k2tog. (23 sts)

Row 17: Knit.

Row 18: Ssk, k to last st. (22 sts)

Row 19: K to last 2 sts, k2tog. (21 sts)

Row 20: Knit.

Row 21: Ssk, k to last 2 sts, k2tog. (19 sts)

Row 22: Ssk, k to last 2 sts, k2tog. (17 sts)

Row 23: Ssk, k to last 2 sts, k2tog. (15 sts)

Row 24: Ssk, k to last 2 sts, k2tog. (13 sts)

Row 25: Ssk, k to last 2 sts, k2tog. (11 sts)

Row 26: Ssk, k to last 2 sts, k2tog. (9 sts)

Row 27: K to last 2 sts, k2tog. (8 sts)

Row 28: BO 4, k to last 2 sts, k2tog. (3 sts)

BO remaining sts. Fasten off, leaving a long tail for sewing.

WAVY LEAF

CO 2 sts.

Row 1: Knit.

Row 2: Kfb twice. (4 sts)

Row 3: K to last st, kfb. (5 sts)

Row 4: Knit.

Row 5: Kfb, k to last st, kfb. (7 sts)

Row 6: Knit.

Row 7: Knit.

Row 8: Repeat row 5. (9 sts)

Row 9: Knit.

Row 10: Knit.

Row 11: Kfb, k to end. (10 sts)

Row 12: Kfb, k to end. (11 sts)

Row 13: Knit.

Row 14: K to last 2 sts, k2tog. (10 sts)

Row 15: Knit.

Row 16: K to last st, kfb. (11 sts)

Row 17: K to last st, kfb. (12 sts)

Row 18: Knit.

Row 19: Kfb, k to end. (13 sts)

Row 20: Ssk, k to end. (12 sts)

Row 21: Knit.

Row 22: Kfb, k to end. (13 sts)

Row 23: Ssk, k to end. (12 sts)

Row 24: Knit.

Row 25: Kfb, k to end. (13 sts)

Row 26: Ssk, k to end. (12 sts)

Row 27: Knit.

Row 28: Kfb, k to last 2 sts, k2tog. (12 sts)

Row 29: Knit.

Row 30: K to last st, kfb. (13 sts)

Row 31: Knit.

Row 32: Knit.

Row 33: Ssk, k to last 2 sts, k2tog. (11 sts)

Row 34: Knit.

Row 35: Knit.

Row 36: Ssk, k to end. (10 sts)

Row 37: Ssk, k to last 2 sts, k2tog. (8 sts)

Row 38: Knit.

Row 39: K to last 2 sts, k2tog. (7sts)

Row 40: K to last 2 sts, k2tog. (6 sts)

Row 41: K to last 2 sts, k2tog. (5 sts)

Row 42: K to last 2 sts, k2tog. (4 sts)

Row 43: Knit.

Row 44: K to last 2 sts, k2tog. (3 sts)

Row 45: K to last 2 sts, k2tog. (2 sts)
Row 46: K2tog.
Break yarn, leaving a long tail for sewing. Pull yarn through remaining loop.

OVAL LEAF

CO 3 sts.
Row 1: Knit.
Row 2: Kfb, k1, kfb. (5 sts)
Row 3: Kfb, k to last st, kfb. (7 sts)
Row 4: Kfb, k to last st, kfb. (9 sts)
Row 5: Knit.
Row 6: Knit.
Row 7: Kfb, k to last st, kfb. (11 sts)
Rows 8–9: Knit.
Row 10: Kfb, k to last st, kfb. (13 sts)
Rows 11–21: Knit.
Row 22: Ssk, k to last 2 sts, k2tog. (11 sts)
Row 23: Knit.
Row 24: Knit.
Row 25: K to last 2 sts, k2tog. (10 sts)
Row 26: Ssk, k to end. (9 sts)
Row 27: Ssk, k to end. (8 sts)
Row 28: Knit.
Row 29: Ssk, k to end. (7 sts)
Row 30: Knit.
Row 31: Ssk, k to end. (6 sts)
Row 32: Knit.
Row 33: Ssk, k to end. (5 sts)
Row 34: Knit.
Row 35: Ssk, k to end. (4 sts)
Row 36: Knit.
Row 37: Ssk, k to end. (3 sts)
Row 38: Sl 1, k2tog, psso.
Break yarn, leaving a long tail for sewing, and pull through remaining stitches to fasten off.

STEMS AND VEINS

CO 10 sts. BO to the last st. Place that st on a crochet hook. Holding the yarn to the back side of the leaf and with the front of the leaf facing you, insert hook into the leaf at its base. Catch the yarn on the back side with the hook and pull a loop through to the right side, pulling that loop through the st on the crochet hook. *Insert the hook through the leaf a little farther up and pull another loop up and through the loop already on the hook. Repeat from * to continue to chain stitch up the middle of the leaf almost to the end. Break yarn and pull end up through leaf and through the last st. Weave in ends. Add more chain stitch veins branching off the main central vein, as shown in the photos.

ASSEMBLY

Cut out a template in the shape and size of the desired rug (you can make your template from paper grocery bags cut flat and taped together or from a large piece of paper). Place the template on a flat surface and lay out leaves over it as desired, overlapping them. Pin the leaves to the template to hold them in place. Using the tails of leaves, sew them together everywhere they overlap. Weave in ends.

Retro Variation

YARN

Cascade 220 (100% wool; 220 yd./200 m; 3.5 oz/100g), 2 skeins each of the following colors:

- *Color A:* Celtic Green (9410)
- *Color B:* Olive Heather (9448)
- *Color C:* Mahogany (2454)
- *Color D:* Turtle (2452)
- *Color E:* Spring Meadow (2438)
- *Color F:* Irelande (2429)

NEEDLES

U.S. size 9 (5.5 mm) straight needles

NOTIONS

U.S. size I-9 (5.5 mm) crochet hook
Sewing needle
Sewing thread to match each yarn color
40 by 30 in. (102 by 76 cm) piece of dark green wool fabric

GAUGE

4 sts = I in. (2.5 cm) in garter stitch

FINISHED MEASUREMENTS

40 by 30 in. (102 by 76 cm) oval

LEAF COLORS

Oak Leaf: Color A (veins in color B)
Narrow Leaf: Color B (veins in color A)
Maple Leaf: Color C (veins in color D)
Fan-Shaped Leaf: Color D (veins in color C)
Wavy Leaf: Color E (veins in color F)
Oval Leaf: Color F (veins in color E)

▮ PATTERN

Using two strands of yarn held together, knit at least 5 of each kind of leaf in the colors indicated above, following the instructions on pages 3–6. Add stems and veins as described in the instructions on page 6. Weave in all ends.

ASSEMBLY

Enlarge the template on page 8 600% and cut out. Wash the piece of wool fabric in hot water with high agitation and a cold rinse to lightly felt the fabric. Repeat if needed, then dry the fabric. Pin the template to the fabric and cut out the base shape. Lay the leaves around the outer edge of the oval, overlapping the leaves and allowing some of them to extend past the edge of the oval. Pin in place. Sew the leaves to the base using matching thread.

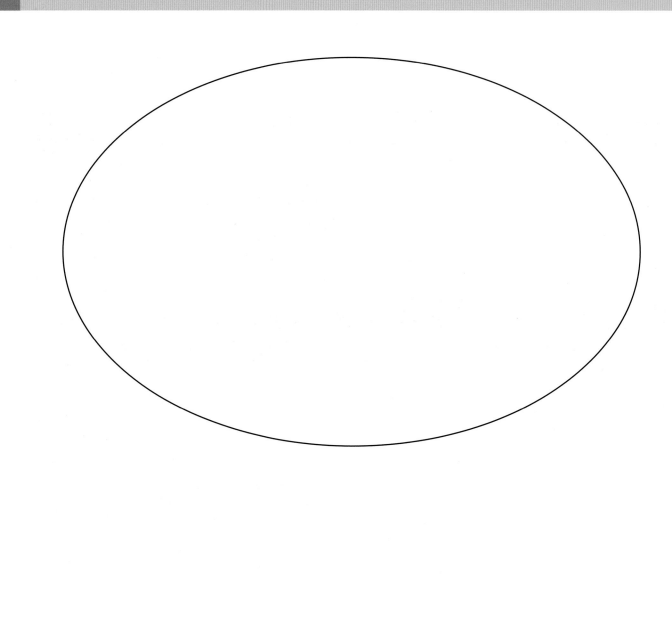

Crazy Combination Rug

As I looked at the skeptical expressions on the faces of my knitting students, I knew what I had asked them to do was outside their comfort zones. "What do you mean, pick two unlikely variegated yarns to knit together?" The instructions were to knit a sample square in the chosen yarns, alternating two rows of one yarn and two rows of the other. And I wasn't just asking them to pick unlikely combinations, but to go out of their way to pick two yarns that clashed.

Everyone was all smiles as they filed in the next week for class. No one could believe how lovely each square turned out!

Inspired by this experience with my students, I knew I had to incorporate it into a rug. You might be skeptical, but as they say, the proof is in the pudding. This rug will be a showstopper with both knitters and non-knitters alike.

◼ NOTES

1. Hold two strands of yarn together throughout the rug.
2. Make sure to use a knitted cast-on, which will make it easier to pick up stitches throughout the rug.
3. In choosing your two variegated yarns, don't try to match. Instead, choose two unlikely yarns for beautiful and surprising results with a watercolor effect.
4. Always slip stitches knitwise throughout pattern.

YARN

Red Heart Super Saver Yarn (100% acrylic; 160 yd./146 m; 3 oz./85 g) and Red Heart Classic Yarn (100% acrylic; 146 yd./134 m; 3 oz./85 g), 2 skeins black and 1 skein each of several different variegated yarns.

Variegated colorways used in sample:
Mistletoe, Platoon, Favorite Jeans, Stars and Stripes, Watercolor, Mexicana, Wildflowers, Shaded Greens, Marrakesh, Purple Tones, Peruvian Print, Zebra, Cherrycola, Wedgewoods, Plum Pudding, Blues, Candy Print, Blacklight, Browns, Primary, Earth and Sky, Artist Print, Melonberry, Razzle, Sedona, Green Tones, Camouflage, Bonbon Print, Banana Berry, Rambling Rose, Seagrass, Urban Cameo, Purples, Painted Desert, Monet, Fall, Cherry Chip, Sherbet Print, Williamsburg, and Bikini.

NEEDLES

U.S. size 9 (5.5 mm) 16-inch circular needles

GAUGE

4 sts = 1 in. (2.5 cm) in garter stitch

FINISHED MEASUREMENTS

36 by 24 in. (91 by 61 cm)

■ PATTERN

DIAMOND 1

With two strands of black held together, CO 25 sts using a knitted cast-on.

Row 1 (WS): K to last st, p1.
Row 2 (RS): Sl 1, k10, Sl 1, k2tog, psso, k to last st, p1.
Row 3 and all odd rows until Row 23: Sl 1, k to last st, p1.
Row 4: Sl 1, k9, Sl 1, k2tog, psso, k to last st, p1.
Row 6: Sl 1, k8, Sl 1, k2tog, psso, k to last st, p1.
Row 8: Sl 1, k7, Sl 1, k2tog, psso, k to last st, p1.
Row 10: Sl 1, k6, Sl 1, k2tog, psso, k to last st, p1.
Row 12: Sl 1, k5, Sl 1, k2tog, psso, k to last st, p1.
Row 14: Sl 1, k4, Sl 1, k2tog, psso, k to last st, p1.
Row 16: Sl 1, k3, Sl 1, k2tog, psso, k to last st, p1.
Row 18: Sl 1, k2, Sl 1, k2tog, psso, k to last st, p1.
Row 20: Sl 1, k1, Sl 1, k2tog, psso, k to last st, p1.
Row 22: Sl 1, Sl 1, k2tog, psso, p1.

Row 23: Sl 1, k1, p1.
Row 24: Sl 1, k2tog, psso.
Break yarn and pull through remaining st.

DIAMOND 2

Make Diamond 2 just like Diamond 1, but do not fasten off at the end; leave the remaining st on the needle.

DIAMOND 3

Keep the last stitch from Diamond 2 on the needle. Using two strands of one variegated yarn and with right side facing, pick up 11 sts on the top left edge of Diamond 2. Pick up 1 more st in the leftmost corner of Diamond 2. (13 sts) With right side facing, pick up 12 sts along the top right edge of diamond 1.

Turn and work row 1 of Diamond 1. Drop first variegated yarn; join another variegated yarn and work rows 2 and 3. Continue to work the same as Diamond 1, alternating 2 rows each of the two variegated yarns until the diamond is completed. (Each stripe of variegated yarn will

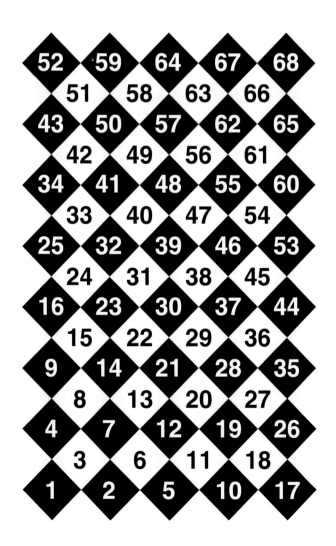

always start with a right-side row.) Leave the last stitch on the needle for the next diamond.

DIAMOND 4

Keep the last stitch from Diamond 3 on the needle and with black yarn and right sides facing, pick up 11 more sts along the top left edge of Diamond 3. Pick up 1 st in the corner. Using a knitted cast-on, cast on 12 sts. Follow directions for Diamond 1, breaking yarn and pulling through last st.

DIAMONDS 5–68

Continue to add diamonds in the order and colors indicated in the chart, starting each diamond by picking up stitches along the top edges of previous diamonds or with a knitted cast-on where there is not a diamond to pick up stitches from. Use a different combination of yarn colors for every variegated diamond.

FINISHING

Weave in ends.

Brick Wall Rug

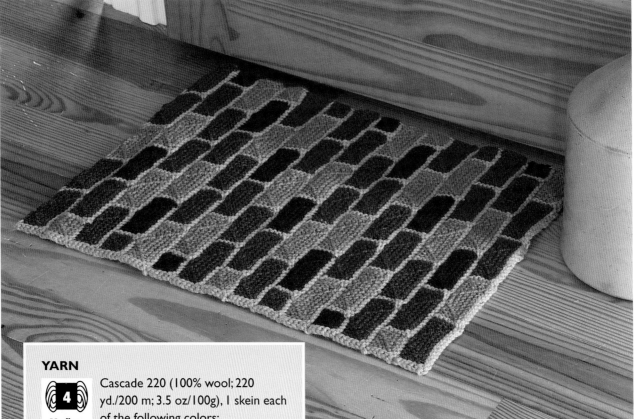

SAMPLE KNITTED BY TERI BUEB

YARN

 4 **Medium**

Cascade 220 (100% wool; 220 yd./200 m; 3.5 oz/100g), 1 skein each of the following colors:

- **Color A:** Nectarine (2451)
- **Color B:** Nutmeg heather (9574)
- **Color C:** Provence (2425)
- **Color D:** Baby rose heather (9442)
- **Color E:** Glamour (2427)
- **Color F:** Flame (2444)

2 skeins of the following:
- **Color G:** Fog Hatt (2442) [grout color]

NEEDLES

U.S. size 9 (5.5 mm) 16-inch circular needles

GAUGE

4 sts = 1 in. (2.5 cm) in garter stitch

FINISHED MEASUREMENTS

22 by 16 in. (56 by 41 cm)

Trompe l'oeil (French for "deceive the eye") refers to any kind of optical illusion. If artists can use this technique in paintings, why not a trompe l'oeil in yarn? That is exactly what we did with this knitted brick wall rug. People visiting your home will do a double take when they see this wall of bricks lying on your floor.

◼ NOTES

1. Hold two strands of yarn together throughout the rug.
2. Follow chart for placement of colors.
3. The slipped stitches should be slipped knitwise throughout.
4. Use a knitted cast-on throughout.

■ PATTERN

BRICK PATTERNS

Full Brick

Row 1 (WS): K20 with color G and break yarn. On the same needle, with brick color, k5, p1. At this point the two colors will be separate. (26 sts)

Row 2 (RS): Sl 1, k4, Sl 1 kwise, k2tog, psso, k10, Sl 1, k2tog, psso, k4, p1. (22 sts)

Row 3: Sl 1, k to last st, p1.

Row 4: Sl 1, k3, Sl 1, k2tog, psso, k8, Sl 1, k2tog, psso, k3, p1. (18 sts)

Row 5: Repeat row 3.

Row 6: Sl 1, k2, Sl 1, k2tog, psso, k6, Sl 1, k2tog, psso, k2, p1. (14 sts)

Row 7: Repeat row 3.

Row 8: Sl 1, k1, Sl 1, k2tog, psso, k4, Sl 1, k2tog, psso, k1, p1. (10 sts)

Row 9: Repeat row 3.

Row 10: Sl 2 (one stitch at a time), k2tog, psso, k2, Sl 1, k2tog, psso, p1. (6 sts)

Row 11: Repeat row 3.

Row 12: *Sl 1, k2tog, psso; repeat from * once; Sl 1, k1, psso.

Pull yarn through last st to fasten off.

Half Brick

Row 1 (WS): K12, p1.

Break off color G and join brick color (following chart).

Row 2 (RS): Sl 1, k4, Sl 1, k2tog, psso, k4, p1. (11 sts)

Row 3: Sl 1, k to last st, p1.

Row 4: Sl 1, k3, Sl 1, k2tog, psso, k3, p1. (9 sts)

Row 5: Repeat row 3.

Row 6: Sl 1, k2, Sl 1, k2tog, psso, k2, p1. (7 sts)

Row 7: Repeat row 3.

Row 8: Sl 1, k1, Sl 1, k2tog, psso, k1, p1. (5 sts)

Row 9: Repeat row 3.

Row 10: Sl 2 (one stitch at a time), k2tog, psso, p1. (3 sts)

Row 11: Sl 1, k1, p1.

Row 12: Sl 1, k2tog, psso.

Break yarn and pull through remaining stitch to fasten off.

SETUP

First Brick

CO 6 sts with color B using a knitted cast-on. On the same needle, CO 20 sts in color G.

Follow the instructions for the full brick.

Following Bricks in Bottom Row

Working to the right of the previous brick, CO 6 sts with the next brick color. CO 13 sts with color G. With G, pick up and knit 1 st in the lower right corner of the previous brick, then pick up and knit 6 sts along the right edge of the previous brick. Make sure the last picked up stitch is in the top right-hand corner.

Follow the instructions for the full brick.

Repeat for the other 3 bricks in the first row.

Half Brick—Beginning of Row

The next row of bricks (and every other row throughout the rug) will start out and end with a half brick, with 4 full-size bricks in between.

Starting at the middle top of the first (far left) brick of the previous row and using color G, pick up and knit 6 sts along the top edge of the brick. Pick up one st in the top left corner. Turn work and, using a knitted cast-on, CO 6 sts.

Follow instructions for the half brick.

Full Brick—Middle of Rug

For next full brick, CO six sts in brick color. Using color G and starting in the middle of the next brick in the row below, pick up and knit 13 sts. Pick up 1 st in the lower right corner of the previous brick. Now pick up and knit 6 more sts along the right edge of the previous brick.

Follow instructions for the full brick.

Repeat for the rest of the full bricks in the row.

Half Brick—End of Row

For rows that end with a half brick, start this brick by picking up and knitting 6 sts on the top right edge of the brick below with color G. Pick up and knit one st in the bottom right corner of the previous brick. Finally pick up and knit 6 sts along the right edge of the previous brick, making sure the last stitch picked up is at the top right corner of the brick.

Follow instructions for the half brick.

Full Brick—Beginning of Row

The third row of bricks (and every other row thereafter) starts with a full brick.

CO 6 sts in brick color. Using color G, pick up and knit 13 st along the top edge of the previous row, starting in the middle of the first full left hand brick and continuing along the top of the half brick. Pick up one st in the upper left hand corner of the half brick below. Turn work and using a knitted cast-on, CO 6 sts.

Follow directions for full brick.

Continue to follow the chart, alternating between rows of full bricks and rows with half bricks at each end, until you have sixteen rows of bricks.

FINISHING

Weave in ends.

Paul Klee Color Play

"Color possesses me. I don't have to pursue it. It will possess me always, I know it. That is the meaning of this happy hour: Color and I are one. I am a painter."

—*Paul Klee*

The challenge was to use as many DMC Tapestry Wool colors as possible in one rug. The first thing that came to mind when thinking about all of those beautiful hues was Swiss-born artist Paul Klee. He was possessed by color, which we can certainly relate to. The other piece that came into the design of this rug was our passion for antique and vintage quilts. Our native Missouri is famous for its postage-stamp quilts, so named because of the diminutive size of each piece. In this rug, Klee's love of color meets postage-stamp quilts to produce a beautiful, vibrant decoration for your floor. For those wanting a challenge, deciding where to place all the colors in this rug is a little like working a jigsaw puzzle.

YARN

DMC Tapestry Wool (100% wool, 8.7 yd./8 m), 1 skein each in 280 different colors
See chart on page 16 for colors used in our rug.

NEEDLES
U.S. size 9 (5.5 mm) straight needles

GAUGE
4 sts = 1 in. (2.5 cm) in garter stitch

FINISHED MEASUREMENTS
34 by 24 in. (86 by 61 cm)

PAUL KLEE COLOR PLAY RUG

DMC Tapestry Wool colors used in the sample.

7207	7202	7823	7715	7369	7344	7285	7489	7223	7348	7107	7316	7453	7017
7369	7033	7347	7520	7196	7488	7400	7138	7558	7769	7518	7202	7303	7313
7452	7364	7138	7597	7176	7348	7797	7895	7179	7322	0003	7520	7408	7436
7488	7151	7031	7063	7282	7790	7110	7971	7124	7466	7316	7606	7200	7770
7244	7107	7317	7771	7927	7202	7406	7799	7024	7300	7435	7369	7204	7518
7457	7192	7018	7226	7398	7452	7174	7108	7042	7798	7266	7453	7692	7300
7396	7033	7946	7067	7010	7703	7119	7057	7549	7463	7135	7046	7318	7168
7726	7141	7432	7306	7767	7302	7300	7387	7215	7896	7492	7273	7121	7542
7604	7165	7068	7433	1530	7999	7133	7632	7323	7055	7364	7196	7846	7241
7132	7474	7450	7107	7041	7371	7504	7029	7171	7713	7845	7399	7345	7011
7064	7238	7423	7260	7032	7063	7701	7025	7001	7422	7167	7173	7450	7813
7922	7394	7058	7236	7760	7746	7704	7920	7490	7386	7521	7026	7626	7078
7510	7711	7548	7802	7280	7505	7060	7470	7740	7020	7223	7288	7106	7487
7326	7739	7319	7439	7351	7599	7268	7949	7139	7500	7484	7715	7772	7151
7191	7514	7217	7359	7243	7853	7363	7400	7431	7234	7922	7375	7143	7314
7493	7193	7678	7579	7444	7618	7199	7317	7341	7605	7598	7499	7166	7347
7313	7320	7268	7519	7207	7382	7851	7144	7021	7489	7245	7678	7558	7147
7420	7303	7598	7479	7435	7311	7141	7205	7890	7783	7122	7038	7255	7946
7212	7485	7221	7245	7344	7469	7800	7017	7503	7127	7429	7465	7769	1535
7488	7860	7138	7506	7285	7603	7353	7919	7459	7861	7284	7640	7725	7823

▦ NOTES

1. Hold two strands of yarn together throughout. Unwind skeins to find both ends of the yarn.
2. All slipped stitches are slipped knitwise.

▦ PATTERN

BASIC SQUARE

Using a knitted cast-on, CO 13 sts. This can be done on either a straight or a circular needle.

Row 1 (WS): K12, p1.
Row 2 (RS): Sl 1, k4, sl 1, k2tog, psso, k4, p1. (11 sts)
Row 3: Sl 1, k to last st, p1.
Row 4: Sl 1, k3, sl 1, k2tog, psso, k3, p1. (9 sts)
Row 5: Sl 1, k to last st, p1.
Row 6: Sl 1, k2, sl 1, k2tog, psso, k2, p1. (7 sts)
Row 7: Sl 1, k to last st, p1.
Row 8: Sl 1, k1, sl 1, k2tog, psso, k1, p1. (5 sts)
Row 9: Sl 1, k to last st, p1.
Row 10: Sl 2, k2tog, psso, p1. (3 sts)
Row 11: Sl 1, k1, p1.
Row 12: Sl 1, k2tog, psso.

Break yarn but leave the remaining stitch on the needle for the next square (unless it is the very last square in the column).

ADDITIONAL SQUARES IN THE FIRST COLUMN

With 1 live st from the previous square on the needle and RS facing, pick up and knit 5 more stitches evenly across the top of the square just finished, working from right to left and making sure to go under both loops. Pick up and knit 1 stitch in the corner loop. (7 sts on needle)

Turn work so that the WS is facing you and CO 6 stitches using a knitted cast-on. (13 sts)

Continue with the basic square pattern, starting with row 1.

Continue to add squares to the column, using a different color for each one, until you have 20 squares altogether. Fasten off the last stitch of the last square in the column.

FIRST SQUARE IN FOLLOWING COLUMNS

Using a knitted cast-on, CO 6 stitches. With RS facing, pick up and knit 1 stitch in the bottom right corner of the first square of the previous column. Pick up and knit 6 more stitches evenly along the right edge of this square, ending in the upper right corner of the square.

Continue with the basic square pattern, starting with row 1. Remember to leave the last stitch on your needle for the next square.

ADDITIONAL SQUARES IN FOLLOWING COLUMNS

With 1 live st from the previous square on the needle and RS facing, pick up and knit 5 more stitches evenly across the top of the square just made. Pick up and knit 1 stitch in the corner, then pick up and knit 6 stitches evenly along the right edge of the neighboring square in the previous column, making sure that the last stitch picked up is at the top of the square.

> **TIP**
> Since there will be a number of ends to work in, we suggest that you work them in as you go.

Continue with the basic square pattern, starting with row 1.

Continue in this manner until there are 14 columns with 20 squares in each column.

Seaside Freeform Rug

SAMPLE KNITTED BY NANCY KLUNDER

MATERIALS
Anything goes as far as yarn weight, texture, and color! You can even use strips of plastic bags and other nontraditional materials. For the main elements in the sample rug, we used medium worsted (weight category 4) yarn.

NEEDLES AND CROCHET HOOKS
Use any and all sizes. Experiment with different size hooks and needles on the same yarn for different effects. For the sample shown here, we used U.S. size 6 (4 mm) knitting needles and a size G-6 (4 mm) crochet hook.

NOTIONS
Sewing needle
Invisible quilter's thread
Tapestry needle
Coat-weight wool fabric for backing (optional)

GAUGE
Gauge is flexible for this pattern

FINISHED MEASUREMENTS
23 by 17 in. (58 by 43 cm)

The hardest thing about making a rug like this is just taking the plunge. Yes, it can be frightening to not work entirely from a pattern. It's a bit like starting a journey unsure of the destination, but freeform knitting is very satisfying once you abandon yourself to it. There are other benefits to this technique—the biggest being that this is a stash-buster, allowing you to use up those little tiny bits of yarn that you don't want to throw away, but don't know what to do with.

▇ NOTE

Although we chose a seaside theme for our rug, you can make your freeform rug with or without a theme. It is a good idea to have a basic color scheme in mind to help unify your rug.

▇ MAKING THE RUG

This rug, like most freeform pieces, is made from a variety of small knitted and crocheted pieces. It is a bit like putting together a puzzle, but you make the puzzle pieces.

If using a wool fabric backing, cut out a piece of wool in the size and shape desired. Pin the pieces to the backing. Sew the pieces together with the yarn tails, and sew them to the backing with matching thread.

If you don't want to use the wool backing, you can build the rug from just the puzzle pieces. Cut out a template the size and shape you want your rug to be from heavy paper. Pin the pieces to this template, moving them around as needed until they fill the whole area you want your rug to cover. When you have covered the paper pattern, sew the pieces together in the arrangement you have developed using the tails from your knitting and crocheting.

We have given you a few patterns to get you started on your freeform adventure. Mix and match these elements, or create your own, to make your own one-of-a-kind rug.

SEA FAN

CO 8 sts using a long-tail cast-on.
Row 1: K2, turn work.
Row 2: Sl 1 purlwise wyif, k1, turn. CO 3 sts. **Note:** *Use a knitted cast-on in row 2 and all following even-numbered rows.*
Row 3: BO 3 sts, k3, turn.
Row 4: Sl 1 purlwise wyif, k3, turn. CO 7 sts.
Row 5: BO 7 sts, k5, turn.
Row 6: Sl 1 purlwise wyif, k5, turn. CO 5 sts.
Row 7: BO 5 sts, k7, turn.
Row 8: Sl 1 purlwise wyif, k7, turn. CO 9 sts.
Row 9: BO 9 sts, k1, turn.
Row 10: Sl 1 purlwise wyif, k1, turn. CO 3 sts.
Row 11: BO 3 sts, k3, turn.
Row 12: Sl 1 purlwise wyif, k3, turn. CO 7 sts.
Row 13: BO 7 sts, k5, turn.
Row 14: Sl 1 purlwise wyif, k5, turn. CO 5 sts.
Row 15: BO 5 sts, k7, turn.
Row 16: Sl 1 purlwise wyif, k7, turn. CO 9 sts.
Row 17: BO 9 sts, k1, turn.
Row 18: Sl 1 purlwise wyif, k1, turn. CO 3 sts.
Row 19: BO 3 sts, k3, turn.
Row 20: Sl 1 purlwise wyif, k3, turn. CO 7 sts.

Row 21: BO 7 sts, k5, turn.
Row 22: Sl 1 purlwise wyif, k5, turn. CO 5 sts.
Row 23: BO 13 sts. Break yarn and work in ends.

BUBBLE

CO 28 sts using a long-tail cast-on. Distribute evenly between three needles and join to work in the round.
Round 1 (RS): Knit.
Round 2 (WS): Purl.
Round 3: K2tog around. (14 sts)
Round 4: Purl.
Round 5: Knit.
Round 6: Purl.
Round 7: K2tog around. (7 sts)
Break yarn and thread through remaining sts. Pull tight and fasten off. Weave in ends or save them to use for sewing pieces together.

LARGE KELP

CO 2 sts.
Row 1: Knit.
Row 2: Kfb twice. (4 sts)
Row 3: Knit.
Row 4: Kfb, k to end. (5 sts)
Row 5: Knit.
Row 6: Kfb, k to end. (6 sts)
Row 7: Knit.
Row 8: Kfb, k to end. (7 sts)
Row 9: Knit.
Row 10: Knit.
Row 11: K to last st, kfb. (8 sts)
Row 12: K to last 2 sts, k2tog. (7 sts)
Row 13: Knit.
Row 14: Kfb, k to end. (8 sts)
Row 15: Knit.
Row 16: K to last 2 sts, k2tog. (7 sts)
Row 17: Knit.
Row 18: Knit.
Row 19: Kfb, k to end. (8 sts)
Row 20: Ssk, k to end. (7 sts)
Row 21: Knit.
Row 22: K to last st, kfb. (8 sts)
Row 23: Knit.
Row 24: Knit.
Row 25: K to last 2 sts, k2tog. (7 sts)
Row 26: Knit.
Row 27: Knit.
Row 28: Knit.
Row 29: Ssk, k to last st, kfb. (7 sts)
Row 30: Knit.
Row 31: Ssk, k to end. (6 sts)

Row 32: Kfb, k to the last 2 sts, k2tog. (6 sts)
Row 33: Knit.
Row 34: K to last 2 sts, k2tog. (5 sts)
Row 35: K to last st, kfb. (6 sts)
Row 36: K to last 2 sts, k2tog. (5 sts)
Row 37: Knit.
Row 38: Knit.
Row 39: Knit.
Row 40: K to last st, kfb. (6 sts)
Row 41: Knit.
Row 42: Knit.
Row 43: K to last 2 sts, k2tog. (5 sts)
Row 44: Knit.
Row 45: Knit.
Row 46: Ssk, k to end. (4 sts)
Row 47: Ssk, k to end. (3 sts)
Row 48: Knit.
Row 49: Ssk, k to end. (2 sts)
BO, break yarn. Weave in ends or save them to use for sewing pieces together.

Using a contrasting color, make a slip knot. Insert crochet hook in the base of the kelp from the front to the back. Pick up the slip knot behind the work and pull it through to the front. Insert the hook through the piece near the edge, about ¼ in. (6 mm) away, yo, and pull yarn through to the front and through the loop on the hook. Continue to work chain stitches along the surface of the piece in this manner around the kelp, keeping the stitches just inside the edge. When complete, break yarn, pull end through last loop on hook to fasten off, and thread tail to the back. Weave in ends or save to use for sewing pieces together.

SMALL KELP

CO 3 sts.
Row 1: Knit.
Row 2: Kfb, k1, kfb. (5 sts)
Row 3: Kfb, k to end. (6 sts)
Row 4: Knit.
Row 5: Knit.
Row 6: Kfb, k to last st, kfb. (8 sts)

Row 7: Knit.

Row 8: Knit.

Row 9: Kfb, k to end. (9 sts)

Row 10: Knit.

Row 11: Knit.

Row 12: Ssk, k to end. (8 sts)

Row 13: Kfb, k to end. (9 sts)

Row 14: Knit.

Row 15: Ssk, k to end. (8 sts)

Row 16: Knit.

Row 17: K to last 2 sts, k2tog. (7 sts)

Row 18: Knit.

Row 19: K to last 2 sts, k2tog. (6 sts)

Row 20: Knit.

Row 21: Knit.

Row 22: Knit.

Row 23: Knit.

Row 24: Kfb, k to end. (7 sts)

Row 25: Knit.

Row 26: Knit.

Row 27: Ssk, k to last st, kfb. (7 sts)

Row 28: Knit.

Row 29: Knit.

Row 30: Knit.

Row 31: Ssk, k to end. (6 sts)

Row 32: Knit.

Row 33: K to last 2 sts, k2tog. (5 sts)

Row 34: Knit.

Row 35: Knit.

Row 36: Ssk, k to end. (4 sts)

Row 37: Knit.

Row 38: K2, k2tog. (3 sts)

Row 39: K1, k2 tog. (2 sts)

BO rem sts, break yarn, and weave in ends or save to use for sewing pieces together.

Embellish with chain stitches around the edge as for the large kelp.

SEA FROND

CO 35 stitches. Knit 3 rows. Bind off.

Take the top two inches of the frond and coil into a spiral. Sew the spiral together.

CROCHETED SEA URCHIN

Ch 3, join with a slip stitch to form a ring.

Row 1: Ch 3. *Wrap yarn 5 times around the hook. Insert hook into ring, yarn over, and draw up a loop (7 loops on hook). Yarn over again and draw yarn through all but 2 loops; yarn over and draw through remaining two loops. Repeat from * 11 or 12 more times. Join with a slip stitch in top chain of beg ch-3. Fasten off.

CROCHETED SPIRAL

Ch 3, join with slip stitch to form ring. Ch 3, work 12 dc in ring. *Do not join.* Work 2 dc in back loop of each ch of beg ch-3 (not ch-3 of ring). Work 2 dc in back loop of first dc of round. Continue around, working 2 double crochet in the back loop of each stitch. Make as large as desired.

COLOR AND TEXTURE

My guess is that if you like to knit, you are a visual and tactile person. When I overhear knitters speak of their latest trip to the yarn store, it is in hushed tones as they try to capture in words the kaleidoscope of colors and myriad of textures that they encountered.

The rugs in this chapter appeal to both the eye and the sense of touch. As far as color goes, I am drawn to bright, bold colors; if you are like me, you will probably be attracted to the Color Wheel Rug, the Hit-and-Miss Rug, or Mondrian Meets Intarsia. But I also love the subtle changes from one color to the next in the Turner Watercolor Welt Rug.

In addition to visual appeal, we also imagined how each rug we designed would feel under bare feet. The textures in the Turner Watercolor Welt Rug, the Hit-and-Miss Rug, and the Giant Cables all feel positively luxurious to our oft-forgotten feet. But don't just believe me. Knit one yourself to try it out!

We hope you will personalize these patterns, changing the colors to match your home or taste. Of course, this goes for any of the patterns in this book—but this chapter is a particularly appropriate place to play with colors.

■ Color Wheel Rug

SAMPLE KNITTED BY LINDA PIETZ

"For the colours diametrically opposed to each other ... are those that reciprocally evoke each other in the eye."

—Johann Wolfgang von Goethe

The color wheel is a way of organizing colors around a circle to show the relationships between them. A color wheel is a very useful tool for learning how to use color to best effect. With this rug, it can also be a beautiful way to display twelve gorgeous shades of color in your home.

■ NOTES

1. Hold two strands of yarn together throughout the rug.
2. The slipped stitches should be slipped purlwise throughout.

■ PATTERN

Begin with a slip knot in waste yarn on the crochet hook. Chain 66 stitches. Using color A and knitting needles, pick up 64 sts through bumps of chain (provisional cast-on). Cut the end of the waste yarn but do not fasten off; secure the live loop at the end of the chain so it doesn't unravel while you're working.

Row 1 (RS): K2, turn.
Row 2 (WS): Sl 1, k1, turn.
Row 3: K4, turn.
Row 4: Sl 1, k3, turn.
Row 5: K6, turn.
Row 6: Sl 1, k5, turn.
Row 7: K8, turn.

YARN

 Cascade 220 (100% wool; 220 yd./200 m; 3.5 oz/100g), 1 skein each in the following colors:

- **Color A:** Dark Plum (8885) [red violet]
- **Color B:** Christmas Red (8895) [red]
- **Color C:** Tiger Lily (9605) [red orange]
- **Color D:** Blaze (9542) [orange]
- **Color E:** California Poppy (7826) [yellow orange]
- **Color F:** Goldenrod (7827) [yellow]
- **Color G:** Primavera (8903) [yellow green]
- **Color H:** Palm (2409) [green]
- **Color I:** Jade (7813) [blue green]
- **Color J:** Kentucky Blue (9485) [blue]
- **Color K:** Blueberry (9464) [blue violet]
- **Color L:** Italian Plum (8886) [violet]

NEEDLES

U.S. size 7 (4.5 mm) 16-inch circular needles

NOTIONS

U.S. size H-8 (5 mm) crochet hook
Small amount of waste yarn in a contrasting color

GAUGE

5 sts = 1 in. (2.5 cm) in garter stitch

FINISHED MEASUREMENTS

31 in. (79 cm) in diameter

Row 8: Sl 1, k7, turn.
Row 9: K10, turn.
Row 10: Sl 1, k9, turn.
Row 11: K12, turn.
Row 12: Sl 1, k11, turn.
Row 13: K14, turn.
Row 14: Sl 1, k13, turn.
Row 15: K16, turn.
Row 16: Sl 1, k15, turn.
Row 17: K18, turn.
Row 18: Sl 1, k17, turn.
Row 19: K20, turn.
Row 20: Sl 1, k19, turn.
Row 21: K22, turn.
Row 22: Sl 1, k21, turn.
Row 23: K24, turn.
Row 24: Sl 1, k23, turn.
Row 25: K26, turn.

Row 26: Sl 1, k25, turn.
Row 27: K28, turn.
Row 28: Sl 1, k27, turn.
Row 29: K30, turn.
Row 30: Sl 1, k29, turn.
Row 31: K32, turn.
Row 32: Sl 1, k31, turn.
Row 33: K34, turn.
Row 34: Sl 1, k33, turn.
Row 35: K36, turn.
Row 36: Sl 1, k35, turn.
Row 37: K38, turn.
Row 38: Sl 1, k37, turn.
Row 39: K40, turn.
Row 40: Sl 1, k39, turn.
Row 41: K42, turn.
Row 42: Sl 1, k41, turn.
Row 43: K44, turn.
Row 44: Sl 1, k43, turn.
Row 45: K46, turn.
Row 46: Sl 1, k45, turn.
Row 47: K48, turn.
Row 48: Sl 1, k47, turn.
Row 49: K50, turn.
Row 50: Sl 1, k49, turn.
Row 51: K52, turn.
Row 52: Sl 1, k51, turn.
Row 53: K54, turn.
Row 54: Sl 1, k53, turn.
Row 55: K56, turn.
Row 56: Sl 1, k55, turn.
Row 57: K58, turn.
Row 58: Sl 1, k57, turn.
Row 59: K60, turn.
Row 60: Sl 1, k59, turn.
Row 61: K62, turn.
Row 62: Sl 1, k61, turn.
Row 63: K64, turn.
Row 64: Sl 1, k63, turn.
Break A and join B.
Repeat rows 1–64.
Break B and join C.

Continue in this pattern, working rows 1–64 with each of the colors in order, from A to L.

When all twelve wedges of the color wheel have been knit, unravel the chain from the provisional cast-on, one stitch at a time, picking up the stitches as you pull the chain out. Holding the right sides together, do a three-needle bind-off with the sts from the provisional cast-on and the sts from the last row of the rug, working with Color L. Weave in ends.

Turner Watercolor Welt Rug

Although he started out painting bucolic landscapes, nineteenth-century painter J. M. W. Turner gradually changed his style to the very abstract, wanting to inspire feeling through color alone. Misunderstood by his contemporaries, since his death he has been the guiding star for generations of artists, including the Impressionists. We hope this rug, with its subtle color changes that play across the welts, inspires good feelings in you every time you look at it.

■ NOTES

1. Hold two strands of yarn together throughout the rug.
2. All the color changes will occur either after a row 6 or a row 10.

■ PATTERN

With two strands of A held together, CO 75 stitches.

Row 1: P1, sl 1 purlwise wyib; repeat to last st, p1.
Row 2: K1, sl 1 purlwise wyif; repeat to last st, k1.
Row 3: Repeat row 1.
Row 4: Repeat row 2.
Row 5: Repeat row 1.
Row 6: Knit.
Row 7: Repeat row 1.

YARN

Cascade 220 (100% wool; 220 yd./200 m; 3.5 oz/100g), I skein each in the following colors:

- *Color A:* Celery (9407)
- *Color B:* Spring Meadow (2438)
- *Color C:* Pear (8412)
- *Color D:* Gold (9463B)
- *Color E:* Mimosa (2436)
- *Color F:* Nectarine (2451)
- *Color G:* Baby Rose Heather (9442)
- *Color H:* Dusty Rose (8114)
- *Color I:* Mauve Heather (9441)
- *Color J:* Light Purple (8420)
- *Color K:* Mystic Purple (2450)
- *Color L:* Montmartre (2423)
- *Color M:* Sapphire Heather (9456)

NEEDLES

U.S. size 9 (5.5 mm) 36-inch circular needles

GAUGE

19 sts = 4 in. (10 cm) in pattern

FINISHED MEASUREMENTS

26 by 17 in. (66 by 43 cm)

Row 8: Repeat row 2.
Row 9: Repeat row 1.
Row 10: Knit.
Repeat rows 1–10 for pattern.
Continue with two strands of A for 6 more rows.
Work 10 rows using one strand each of color A and B.
Work 10 rows using color B.
Work 10 rows using one strand each of color B and C.
Work 10 rows using color C.
Work 10 rows using one strand each of color C and D.
Work 10 rows using color D.
Work 10 rows using one strand each of color D and E.
Work 10 rows using color E.
Work 10 rows using one strand each of color E and F.
Work 10 rows using color F.
Work 10 rows using one strand each of color F and G.
Work **14 rows** using color G.
Work 10 rows using one strand each of color G and H.
Work 10 rows using color H.
Work 10 rows using one strand each of color H and I.
Work 10 rows using color I.

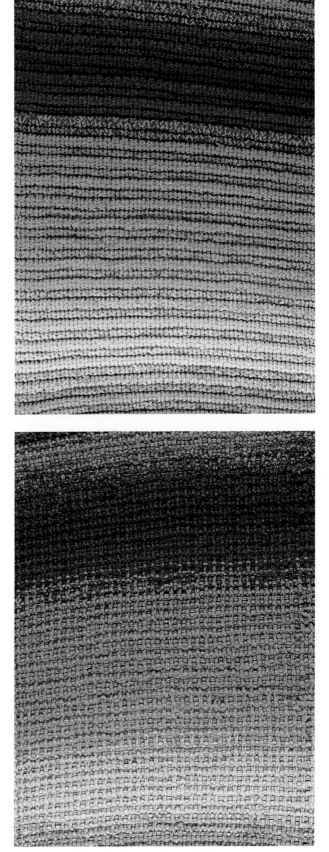

The two sides of this rug have different textures. Either would make an attractive "right" side!

Work 10 rows using one strand each of color I and J.
Work 10 rows using color J.
Work 10 rows using one strand each of color J and K.
Work 10 rows using color K.
Work 10 rows using one strand each of color K and L.
Work 10 rows using color L.

Work 10 rows using one strand each of color L and M.
Work **16 rows** using color M.
Bind off pwise.
Break yarn, leaving a 40-in. (102-cm) tail. Fold bound-off edge to the back and loosely whipstitch down in order to match the beginning of the rug.

Hit-and-Miss Rug

I have always loved randomly created folk fiber arts where it is obvious that the creator just used what was on hand, without worrying about trying to match or coordinate colors or materials. Out of that love for randomness this rug was born. For many years I have taught a scarf version of this rug with knitting students. I would draw from my stash and ask students to bring a skein or two from theirs and we would place these in brown paper lunch bags. After scrambling them up, I had each knitter select a bag to get their scarf going. Once the cast-on was completed, each knitter would return their yarn in its bag and grab another for the next row. This would go on until the scarf was the desired width. Overall, this worked pretty well, but I had to keep an eagle eye on my knitters to be sure

YARN
Scraps of yarn from your stash—any weight and type. For one row you'll need two 8-yard pieces of worsted-weight yarn.

NEEDLES
U.S. size 8 (5 mm) 36-inch circular needles

GAUGE
4.5 sts = 1 in. (2.5 cm) in garter stitch

FINISHED MEASUREMENTS
37 by 21 in. (94 by 53 cm), not including fringe

they didn't peek or squeeze the bag before making their selection. Another great trick the knitters used was to watch where a knitter placed a desirable returning bag, so as to grab it for themselves. True randomness, it seems, is very hard for many people. How about making a matching scarf to go with your rug? But no peeking!

TIPS

- Put your cut pieces of yarn into brown paper lunch sacks, separating the worsteds from the novelty yarns. Alternate randomly grabbing from the worsted pile and the novelty pile. No peeking!
- Put stitch markers every 20 stitches to help you keep track of stitches on the needle, which can sometimes be challenging when knitting with novelty yarns.
- Have a "Rug Bee," with one knitter starting the rug and knitting on it for a week or two and then passing it on to another knitter. Keep passing it around your group until completed. This could be a great group project for a wedding or house-warming gift.
- Have a rug party. In advance, have your group of knitting friends cut 8-yard lengths of assorted yarns for each attendee. Host a rug-beginning party where you all get together, exchange your 8-yard bits, and begin your rugs. Have a completion party as well!

NOTES

1. This rug will be knit lengthwise. The tails at the beginning and end of each row will become the fringe on the ends of the rug.
2. For stability, knit every other row with two strands of worsted-weight yarn held together, alternating with rows of novelty yarns. When using lighter-weight yarns, such as sock yarn, hold even more strands together.

PATTERN

Leaving a 12-inch tail at the beginning, CO 120 stitches using a knitted cast-on. Cut yarn, leaving another 12-inch tail.

Row 1 and all succeeding rows: Knit, leaving a 12-inch tail at each end of the row.

When desired width is reached, bind off loosely, using size 9 or 10 needles.

Divide the tails at the ends of the rug into small bundles and tie an overhand knot in each bundle. Trim fringe to desired length.

Variation

SAMPLE KNITTED BY LOUISE ISAACSON

Make the rug in the same way, with the same random yarn-selection pattern, but only include yarns from one color family or color scheme (such as all blues or all reds) in your pool to grab from.

Mondrian Meets Intarsia

YARN

5 Bulky Cascade 128 (100% wool, 128 yd./117 m; 3.5 oz./100 g), in the following colors:

- **3 skeins Bright Red** (8414)
- **2 skeins Black** (8555)
- **2 skeins White** (8505)
- **1 skein Silver Grey** (8401)
- **1 skein Gold** (9463B)
- **1 skein Blue Velvet** (7818)

NEEDLES

U.S. size 5 (3.75 mm) 24-inch circular needles

NOTIONS

Bobbins (optional)

GAUGE

4.5 sts = 1 in. (2.5 cm) in stockinette stitch

FINISHED MEASUREMENTS

26 by 23 in. (66 by 58 cm)

P iet Mondrian was a rather quirky artistic genius. He proclaimed nature "a damned wretched affair" and chose instead to create precise, mechanically ordered paintings in black, white, gray, and primary colors. Perhaps next to the Mona Lisa, Mondrian's geometric paintings are among the most imitated. As I always like to say, if they make a shower curtain out of your artwork, you have arrived.

A bit of a control freak, Mondrian decorated his entire studio to resemble one of his paintings. The only decoration was an artificial red flower with its leaves painted white, since to him green was a banned color. Even if you have a bit of green in your room, it's okay to add your own knitted knock-off of Mr. Mondrian's work. We won't tell him about the green.

■ NOTES

1. Small amounts of colored yarn can be held on bobbins or wound into balls.

2. When working across the row and changing from one color to the other, make sure to twist the two yarns as follows: bring the previously knit yarn over and to the left of the new color. Bring the new color under and to the right of the old one.

3. All black stitches are worked in seed stitch and all other colors are worked in stockinette stitch.

■ PATTERN

CO 100 sts.

Row 1 (RS): With black, *k1, p1; repeat to end.

Row 2 (WS): With black, *p1, k1; repeat to end.

Row 3: Repeat row 1.

Row 4: Repeat row 2.

Row 5: Repeat row 1.

Row 6: With black, [p1, k1] twice; with gray, p25; with black, [k1, p1] twice; with red, p63; with black, [p1, k1] twice.

Row 7: With black, [k1, p1] twice; with red, k63; with black, [p1, k1] twice; with gray, k25; with black, [k1, p1] twice.

Rows 8–40: Repeat rows 6–7, ending with a repeat of row 6.

Row 41: With black, [k1, p1] twice; with red, k63; with black, *p1, k1, repeat from * to last st, p1.

Row 42: With black, *p1, k1, repeat from * to last st of black section, p1; with red, p63; with black, [p1, k1] twice.

Row 43: Repeat row 41.

Row 44: Repeat row 42.

Row 45: Repeat row 41.

Row 46: With black, [p1, k1] twice; with white, p25; with black, [k1, p1] twice; with red, p63; with black, [p1, k1] twice.

Row 47: With black, [k1, p1] twice; with red, k63; with black, [p1, k1] twice; with white, k25; with black, [k1, p1] twice.

Rows 48–115: Repeat rows 46–47.

Row 116: Repeat row 2.

Row 117: Repeat row 1.

Row 118: Repeat row 2.

Row 119: Repeat row 1.

Row 120: Repeat row 2.

Row 121: With black, [k1, p1] twice; with white, k15; with black, [p1, k1] twice; with white, k44; with black, [p1, k1] twice; with blue, k25; with black, [k1, p1] twice.

Row 122: With black, [p1, k1] twice; with blue, p25; with black, [k1, p1] twice; with white, p44; with black, [k1, p1] twice; with white, p15; with black, [p1, k1] twice.

Rows 123–141: Repeat rows 121–122, ending with a repeat of row 121.

Row 142: With black, [p1, k1] twice; with blue, p25; with black, [k1, p1] twice; with white, p44; with black, *k1, p1, repeat from * to last st, k1.

Row 143: With black, *k1, p1, repeat from * to last st of black section, k1; with white, k44; with black, [p1, k1] twice; with blue, k25; with black, [k1, p1] twice.

Row 144: Repeat row 142.

Row 145: Repeat row 143.

Row 146: Repeat row 142.

Row 147: With black, [k1, p1] twice; with yellow, k15; with black, [p1, k1] twice; with white, k44; with black, [p1, k1] twice; with blue, k25; with black, [k1, p1] twice.

Row 148: With black, [p1, k1] twice; with blue, p25; with black, [k1, p1] twice; with white, p44; with black, [k1, p1] twice; with yellow, p15; with black, [p1, k1] twice.

Rows 149–175: Repeat rows 147–148, ending with a repeat of row 147.

Row 176: Repeat row 2.

Row 177: Repeat row 1.

Row 178: Repeat row 2.

Row 179: Repeat row 1.

Row 180: Repeat row 2.

BO in pattern.

FINISHING

Weave in ends.

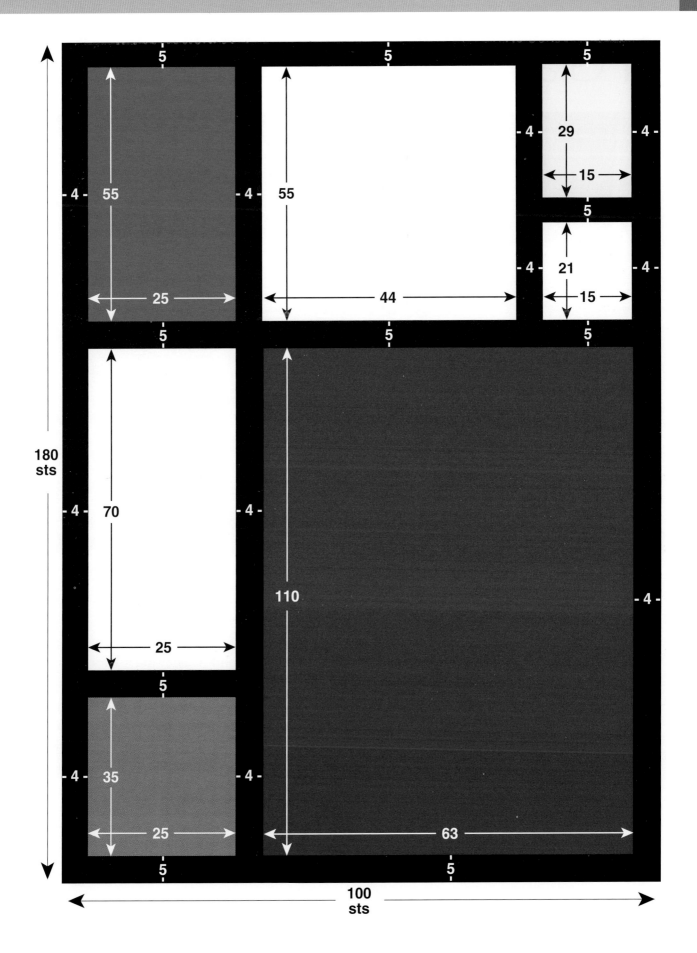

Giant Cables

SAMPLE KNITTED BY YARDA HANSEN

YARN

Cascade 128 (100% superwash merino wool, 128 yd./117 m; 3.5 oz./100 g), 8 skeins Doeskin Heather (8012)

NEEDLES

U.S. size 11 (8 mm) 36-inch circular needles

NOTIONS

Cable needle
7 stitch markers

GAUGE

3 sts = 1 in. (2.5 cm)

FINISHED MEASUREMENTS

31 by 18 in. (79 by 46 cm)

My love affair with Aran sweaters goes way back into my childhood. Our parents took a trip to Europe, leaving my sisters and me behind. They did ask for souvenir requests, and even at a tender age, what I wanted most was a hand-knit Aran sweater and an embroidered blouse from Germany. Imagine my delight when they returned with the requested gifts! I won't complain too much that they got a sweater that looked more like a dress on me.

Fast forward to my college years. They say that you should never knit a sweater for a boyfriend until you get the ring. Did I heed that warning? Absolutely not. I knitted Mr. X an Aran sweater, taking meticulous measurements.

But when it was all done, he was unhappy with the length of the sleeves. All of that hard work went into a drawer. As time went on, Mr. X and I parted ways. I wonder what ever happened to that beautiful sweater?

Despite my roller-coaster past with Aran sweaters, I knew we needed to include a rug version in the book. Thus the Giant Cables rug was born. I can't advise you on whether the boyfriend sweater curse applies to rugs or not.

■ NOTE

Hold two strands of yarn together throughout the rug.

SPECIAL STITCHES

C6B: Slip next 3 sts onto cable needle and hold in back of work, k3, k3 sts from cable needle.
C6F: Slip next 3 sts onto cable needle and hold in front of work, k3, k3 sts from cable needle.

■ PATTERN

CO 70 sts using a long-tail cast-on.
Row 1: K2, p2, k2, pm, p4, pm, k12, pm, p4, pm, k18, pm, p4, pm, k12, pm, p4, pm, k2, p2, k2.
Row 2: P2, k2, p2, k4, p12, k4, p18, k4, p12, k4, p2, k2, p2.
Row 3: P2, k2, p2, p4, k12, p4, C6B 3 times, p4, k12, p4, p2, k2, p2.
Row 4: K2, p2, k2, k4, p12, k4, p18, k4, p12, k4, k2, p2, k2.
Row 5: K2, p2, k2, p4, k12, p4, k18, p4, k12, p4, k2, p2, k2.
Row 6: P2, k2, p2, k4, p12, k4, p18, k4, p12, k4, p2, k2, p2.
Row 7: P2, k2, p2, p4, C6B, C6F, p4, k3, C6F twice, k3, p4, C6B, C6F, p4, p2, k2, p2.
Row 8: K2, p2, k2, k4, p12, k4, p18, k4, p12, k4, k2, p2, k2.
Repeat rows 1 through 8 until rug measures approximately 30 in. (76 cm) BO in pattern.

FINISHING

Weave in ends.

CHAPTER 3 OPEN RUGS

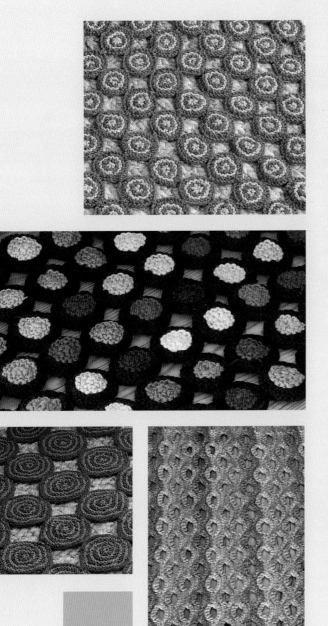

Perhaps it is counterintuitive to have "holey" rugs—but to me, there is something appealing about allowing the floor beneath to peek through and become a visual part of the rug.

Another great advantage to these rugs is that many of them, like their cousins in Chapter 1, are basically modular rugs. Making a rug in smaller sections makes it easier to track your progress and gives you a sense of accomplishment every time you complete a module. Plus, they are great to bring along with you as "emergency knitting."

■ Knitted Penny Rug

YARN

DMC Tapestry Wool (100% wool, 8.7 yd./8 m) in black and a variety of bright colors

NEEDLES
U.S. size 9 (5.5 mm) double-pointed needles

NOTIONS
Tapestry needle

GAUGE
One penny = 1¾ in. (4.4 cm) in diameter

FINISHED MEASUREMENTS
24 by 17 in. (61 by 43 cm)

In the mid-1800s, our thrifty ancestors cut circles from worn wool garments, using coins or other circular items as templates. Small circles were buttonhole-stitched to larger ones and then sewn together or stitched to a backing to create colorful rugs. Recreating those beautiful penny rugs in knitting is fun and easy. It takes practically no time to knit up one penny. The other nice thing about this rug is that it is a great portable project—perfect for a road trip.

▓ PATTERN

PENNY

With two strands of black held together and using a long-tail cast-on, CO 28 sts. Distribute evenly among three needles. Join into round, being careful not to twist sts.

Round 1: Purl.

Round 2: Knit.

Round 3: Purl. Break black and join 2 strands of CC held together.

Round 4: K2tog around. (14 sts)

Round 5: Purl.

Round 6: Knit.

Round 7: Purl.

Round 8: K2tog around. (7 sts)

Break yarn and thread through remaining sts, pulling tight, to fasten off.

Weave in all ends except the tail on the outside edge. You will use this when sewing the pennies together.

Make 70 pennies, using a different color for the CC in each one.

FINISHING

Take two pennies and hold with right sides together. Sew together through 2 stitches on the outside edge, using the tail from one of the pennies. Open up the seam so you have two pennies joined on one side.

Hold the next penny together with one of the first two with right sides together. Count to the 13th and 14th stitches from the previous seam and sew those two stitches together through the edges of both pennies.

Continue sewing on pennies until you have a strip of 10 pennies. Make 6 more strips of 10 pennies.

Finally, sew the strips of pennies together. There should be 5 stitches in between each pair of 2-stitch seams.

Weave in all remaining ends.

Buttonhole Rug

SAMPLE KNITTED BY IRENE BERGH

YARN

5
Bulky

Cascade 128 (100% superwash merino wool, 128 yd./117 m; 3.5 oz./100 g), 1 skein each of the following colors:

- **Color A:** Summer Sky Heather (9452)
- **Color B:** Doeskin Heather (8012)
- **Color C:** Turtle (2452)
- **Color D:** Silver Grey (8401)

NEEDLES
U.S. size 7 (4.5 mm) 24-inch circular needles

GAUGE
5 sts = 1 in. (2.5 cm) in garter stitch

FINISHED MEASUREMENTS
28 by 20 in. (71 by 51 cm)

Don't ask me why, but there is something that I find intriguing about a rug with deliberate holes in it. This rug makes a statement while allowing your beautiful hardwood, carpeted, or tile floor to peek through, making the surface underneath it a part of the look of this rug. Don't like the different colored stripes? Make it in just one color for an entirely different look, where the texture is what makes the statement, along with those intentional holes.

SPECIAL STITCH

Buttonhole: To make a buttonhole, sl 1 wyif, sl 1 wyib, pass first slipped st over second; [sl 1 wyif, pass prev slipped st over this one, sl 1 wyib, pass prev slipped st over this one] twice, sl 1 wyif, pass prev slipped st over this one. Slip the last stitch back onto the left-hand needle. Turn work. Using a knitted cast-on, CO 6 sts. Turn work, k6.

■ PATTERN

Using color A, CO 102 stitches.

Rows 1–3: Knit.

Row 4 (WS): K3, purl to last 3 sts, k3.

Row 5 (RS): Knit.

Row 6: Knit.

Row 7: K3, *work buttonhole, k4; repeat from * 8 more times; work buttonhole, k3. (10 buttonholes; 102 sts) Break off color A and join color B.

Row 8: Repeat row 4.

Row 9: Knit.

Row 10: Knit.

Row 11: K8, *work buttonhole, k4; repeat from * 8 more times, k4. (9 buttonholes; 102 sts)

Break off color B and join color C.

Rows 12–15: Repeat rows 4–7.

Break off color C and join color D.

Rows 16–19: Repeat rows 8–11.

Break off color D and join color A.

Rows 20–147: Repeat rows 4–19 eight more times. Do not break off color D at the end of the last repeat.

Rows 148–150: With color D, knit. BO. Weave in ends.

TIP

In rows 7 and 11, you can help yourself keep track of your stitches by placing a marker at the beginning of every repeat (every time you get to *). You should end up with 10 sts between each pair of markers. Remove the markers after the row is completed.

You can bring your creativity to bear not only in how you make your rugs, but also in how you display them. This rug would also make a great placemat—or make it a little thinner and longer for a table runner!

Goin' Round in Circles

SAMPLE KNITTED BY DIANA WESTIN AND DEBI STALDER

YARN

 Cascade 128 (100% superwash merino wool, 128 yd./117 m; 3.5 oz./100 g)

■ *6 skeins Color A:* Lichen (9338)
■ *4 skeins Color B:* Straw (4010)

NEEDLES
U.S. size 7 (4.5 mm) double-pointed needles

NOTIONS
Tapestry needle

GAUGE
One circle = 4 in. (10 cm) in diameter

FINISHED MEASUREMENTS
43 by 32 in. (109 by 81 cm)

Circles are everywhere in our world. Think of tree rings or ripples in a pond. The tires on our car that get us to where we want to go, while we steer that same automobile with yet another circle. But in our fast-paced world, it can sometimes feel like *we* are going around in circles. So stop, sit down, and knit awhile on this rug, stepping off that circular merry-go-round we call modern life.

■ NOTE
Make sure to bring yarn not being used to the wrong side of your knitting. Do not twist yarn when changing from one color to the other.

PATTERN

CIRCLE

Using color A and a long-tail cast-on, CO 56 sts. Join in the round, being careful not to twist sts.

Round 1: With color A, purl.

Drop color A (but do not break off); join color B.

Round 2: With color B, *k2, k2tog; repeat from * around. (42 sts)

Round 3: Purl.

Drop color B and pick up color A.

Round 4: Knit.

Round 5: Purl.

Drop color A and pick up color B.

Round 6: *K1, k2tog; repeat from * around. (28 sts)

Round 7: Purl.

Drop color B and pick up color A.

Round 8: Knit.

Round 9: Purl.

Drop color A and pick up color B.

Round 10: K2tog around. (14 sts)

Round 11: Purl.

Drop color B and pick up color A.

Round 12: Knit.

Round 13: Purl.

Break off color A and pick up color B.

Round 14: K2tog around. (7 sts)

Cut yarn, leaving a 6-inch tail. Use a tapestry needle to draw the tail through the remaining 7 sts. Pull tight to fasten off. Weave in ends.

Make 70 circles.

FINISHING

Take circles and hold them with right sides together. Sew together through 4 stitches on the outside edge with color A. Open up the seam so you have two circles joined on one side.

Hold the next circle together with one of the first two with right sides together. Sew the new pair of circles together opposite the first seam (there should be 24 sts in between the two seams). Continue adding circles until you have a strip of 10 circles. Make 6 more strips in the same way.

Finally, sew the strips of circles together, placing the new seams so there are 10 stitches in between each pair of 4-stitch seams.

Weave in all ends.

Mini-Circle Variation

YARN

Cascade 128 (100% superwash merino wool, 128 yd./117 m; 3.5 oz./100 g)

■ *3 skeins Color A:* Sapphire (9332)
■ *2 skeins Color B:* Silver Grey (8401)

NEEDLES

U.S. size 7 (4.5 mm) double-pointed needles

GAUGE

One circle = 1¾ in. (4.4 cm) in diameter

FINISHED MEASUREMENTS

23 in. (58 cm) square

▩ NOTE

Make sure to bring yarn to the wrong side when not in use. Do not twist yarns when changing from one color to the next.

▩ PATTERN

CIRCLE

Using color A and a long-tail cast-on, CO 28 sts. Join into round, making sure not to twist sts.

Round 1: Purl.

Round 2: Knit.

Drop color A (do not break off) and join color B.

Round 3: P2tog around. (14 sts)

Round 4: Knit.

Drop color B and pick up color A.

Round 5: Purl.

Round 6: Knit.

Break off color A and join color B.

Round 7: P2tog around. (7 sts)

Break off color B, leaving a 6-in. (15-cm) tail. Use a tapestry needle to thread the tail through the remaining sts. Pull tight to fasten off. Weave in ends.

Make 81 circles.

FINISHING

Assemble the rug as for the larger version of the rug, but sew seams 2 sts long (instead of 4), with 5 sts in between each pair of seams (instead of 10). Make the rug 9 circles by 9 circles.

"GREEN" RUGS FROM REPURPOSED MATERIALS

How could we not have a chapter like this in our book, especially when so many things around us can find new life as a rug? We all want to be better stewards of our planet, and our crafting can be part of that effort. And I love the idea of taking something that is a little care-worn or outdated and transforming it into something useful again.

"Green" living may be a relatively recent effort, but repurposing is a very old tradition. For our ancestors, repurposing was a way of life. Imagine being one of those brave pioneers who trekked out west to seek a better life. Only bare necessities could make the trip. Running to the nearest box store wasn't an option. These self-reliant stalwarts had to make do with what was on hand.

With that history (and all the wastage in our modern society) in mind we offer you some ideas for beautiful rugs that give unwanted items new life while paying homage to our brave ancestors. I think they would be pleased.

■ String It Up Rug

YARN

Red Heart Creme de la Crème (100% combed cotton; 2.5 oz./71 g; 130 yd./119 m), 4 skeins in Scarlet

NEEDLES

U.S. size 7 (4.5 mm) 36-inch circular needles

NOTIONS

Tapestry needle

OTHER MATERIALS

Hand-dyed wool fabric, ⅝ yard (60 in. wide) each in red orange, yellow orange, yellow green, blue green, blue violet, and red violet

GAUGE

4 sts = 1 in. (2.5 cm) in garter stitch

FINISHED MEASUREMENTS

36 by 24 in. (91 by 61 cm)

Our thrifty ancestors were really the first recyclers. Faced with limited resources, they found creative solutions for covering their dirt or rough-hewn wood floors. When a work shirt or dress came to the end of its life as a garment, they cut it into strips and made a rug. Our modern version is very much like theirs. Fortunately, we don't have dirt floors and rough-hewn wood has given way to beautiful hardwoods with smooth finishes. But no matter what surface you place it on, this rug will no doubt feel as good on the feet as it did to those of a bygone era.

■ PREPARING THE WOOL FABRIC

Cut your wool fabric into ½ by 3 in. (1.2 by 7.5 cm) strips. Toss your cut strips together like a salad to mix the colors up.

Thread your yarn through a tapestry needle and string the wool strips onto the yarn by inserting the needle through the middle of each strip. Start with a comfortable number of strips; as you knit the rug, you will need to periodically break the yarn to string on more pieces of wool. It works best to do this at the edge of the rug.

■ PATTERN

CO 73 sts.

Row 1 (RS): Knit.

Row 2 (WS): *K1, bring up a piece of wool next to the needle, k1; repeat from * to last st, k1. The strips of wool will automatically go to the right side (facing away from you).

Repeat rows 1–2 until piece measures 36 in. (91 cm) or desired length.

Knit one more row.

BO loosely. Weave in yarn ends.

■ T-Shirt Variation

T-shirts might be the modern-day equivalent of the woolen dresses and pants that our ancestors used to make rugs out of. Wool fabric can be hard to find, but many of us have drawers full of old T-shirts that are starting to wear out but that we can't bring ourselves to throw away. This rug is a great way to put them to use.

Cut the T-shirts into strips just like with the wool fabric. (A rotary cutter and cutting mat can be a big help in this process.) String a comfortable number of strips onto your yarn and knit the rug just like in the other variation.

YARN

 4 Medium Red Heart Super Saver Yarn (100% acrylic, 160 yd./146 m; 3 oz./85 g), 1 skein black

OTHER MATERIALS

About 8 T-shirts in dark colors.

FINISHED MEASUREMENTS

29 by 20 in. (74 by 51 cm)

Have a Heart

MATERIALS
7 or 8 red T-shirts without side
   seams

NEEDLES
U.S. size 17 (12.75 mm) 36-inch
circular needles

GAUGE
5 sts = 2 in. (5 cm) in garter stitch

FINISHED MEASUREMENTS
27 by 26 in. (69 by 66 cm)

I have a confession to make: I'm not a girly girl, but I love hearts. Not cutesy hearts, but fun, funky hearts like those found in Jim Dine's paintings. I'm sure I am not alone in my fascination with this ideograph. The idea of the heart as a symbol of love goes back to the middle ages. So we just had to have a heart-shaped rug in this book to satisfy the love we all share, whether young or young at *heart*. (Sorry, I couldn't resist that one.) Although we used red T-shirts for our rug, there's no reason you couldn't use a different color—blue, for example—or a mixture of colors.

■ PREPARING THE T-SHIRTS

Lay a T-shirt out flat and cut off the bottom hem. Cut ½ in. (1.2 cm) strips across the shirt all the way up to the underarms. Pull on the loops to stretch them out. Repeat with the other shirts. You will probably need about 7 or 8 adult large T-shirts.

To join loops together, insert one loop (we'll call it loop B) into another (loop A). Now take the end of loop B that you put through loop A, and bring it around and back through the other end of loop B. Pull tight. Insert a new loop into the end of loop B and repeat the joining process. Continue to join loops, rolling the loop yarn into a ball as you go.

■ NOTE

All slipped stitches will be slipped knitwise.

■ PATTERN

LOBES

Using a knitted cast-on, CO 16 sts. **Note:** *You will be knitting the upper lobes of the heart using short rows.*
Row 1: K2, turn.
Row 2: Sl 1, k1, turn.
Row 3: K4, turn.
Row 4: Sl 1, k3, turn.
Row 5: K6, turn.
Row 6: Sl 1, k5, turn.
Row 7: K8, turn.
Row 8: Sl 1, k7, turn.
Row 9: K10, turn.
Row 10: Sl 1, k9, turn.
Row 11: K12, turn.
Row 12: Sl 1, k11, turn.
Row 13: K14, turn.
Row 14: Sl 1, k13, turn.
Row 15: K16, turn.
Row 16: Sl 1, k15, turn.
Repeat rows 1–16 five more times. Put live stitches on a holder and set aside.
Make a second lobe like the first.
To join the lobes, knit across the 16 stitches of one lobe, then pick up and knit 17 stitches across the rest of edge of the lobe, for a total of 33 stitches on the first lobe. With the same looper yarn, knit across the 16 live stitches of the other lobe, then pick up and knit 16 stitches on the same lobe. Turn. (65 sts)

BODY AND POINT OF HEART

Row 1: K to last st, p1.
Row 2: Sl 1, k30, sl 1, k2tog, psso, k30, p1. (63 sts)
Row 3: Sl 1, k to last st, p1.
Rows 4–59: Repeat rows 2–3. (7 sts at the end of row 59)
Row 60: Sl 1, k1, sl 1, k2tog, psso, k1, p1. (5 sts)
Row 61: Sl 1, k to last st, p1.
Row 62: Sl 2, k2tog, psso, p1. (3 sts)
Row 63: Sl 1, k1, p1.
Row 64: Sl 1, k2tog, psso.
Pull yarn through remaining stitch to fasten off.

FINISHING

Weave in ends.

Holey T-Shirt Rug

SAMPLE KNITTED BY LINDA LEMAN

MATERIALS
About 7 white T-shirts without side
  seams

NEEDLES
U.S. size 17 (12.75 mm) 24-inch circular
needles

GAUGE
2 sts = 1 in. (2.5 cm) in 2 x 2 ribbing
  (k2, p2)

FINISHED MEASUREMENTS
28 by 16 in. (71 by 41 cm)

I've just given up! My husband looks great five days a
week, but when the weekend comes around, it's
fashion felony time. He will wear his T-shirts until
they resemble swiss cheese. Salvaging them before they
get to that point has given me an opportunity to repurpose those T-shirts into fabulous rugs that have intentional holes in them.

This quick-knit rug can be made in any size and
length desired. Prepping the T-shirts takes longer than
the actual knitting. It makes a great rug anywhere, but
would certainly find a happy home in a teenage boy's
room or a man cave.

▓ PREPARING THE T-SHIRTS

Lay out a shirt flat and cut off the bottom hem. Starting anywhere on the bottom edge, cut up into the shirt on a gentle diagonal until you have a strip that is 1 in. (2.5 cm) wide. Continue cutting around and around the T-shirt in a spiral, keeping the strip a constant width. When you get to the arms, taper the strip off to a point. Pull on the T-shirt strip to stretch it out, then roll into a ball. Repeat with the other shirts, sewing the ends together when you join a new strip to the ball. Our example took about 7 large shirts, but this can vary, depending on the size of the shirts and what size rug you want to make.

▓ PATTERN

CO 34 stitches (or any multiple of 8 sts plus 2).

Row 1: *P2, k2; repeat from * to last 2 sts, p2.

Row 2: *K2, p2; repeat from * to last 2 sts, k2.

Row 3: *P2, k1, yo, k1, p2, k2; repeat from * to last 2 sts, p2

Row 4: *K2, p2, k2, p3; repeat from * to last 2 sts, k2.

Row 5: *P2, k3, p2, k2; repeat from * to last 2 sts, p2.

Row 6: Repeat row 4.

Row 7: Repeat row 5.

Row 8: Repeat row 4.

Row 9: *P2, k1, drop next stitch all the way down to the yo in row 3, k1, p2, k2; repeat from * to last 2 sts, p2.

Row 10: Repeat row 2.

Row 11: *P2, k2, p2, k1, yo, k1; repeat from * to last 2 sts, p2.

Row 12: *K2, p3, k2, p2; repeat from * to last 2 sts, k2.

Row 13: *P2, k2, p2, k3; repeat from * to last 2 sts, p2.

Row 14: Repeat row 12.

Row 15: Repeat row 13.

Row 16: Repeat row 12.

Row 17: *P2, k2, p2, k1, drop next stitch all the way down to the yo in row 11, k1; repeat from * to last 2 sts, p2.

Row 18: Repeat row 2.

Repeat rows 1–18 three more times or until rug reaches desired length.

BO loosely.

FINISHING

Work in ends.

■ Wool Gizzard Rug

SAMPLE KNITTED BY PHYLLIS EISENBERG

MATERIALS
Wool gizzards in varying lengths and colors tied together with overhand knots with 2-in. (5-cm) tails and rolled into a ball.

NEEDLES
U.S. size 11 (8 mm) 24-inch circular

GAUGE
3 sts = 1 in. (2.5 cm) in garter stitch

FINISHED MEASUREMENTS
30 by 20 in. (76 by 51 cm)

Gizzards? You're probably wondering where the name for this rug comes from. Traditional rug hookers use these little strips of wool to make hooked rugs; in the spirit of repurposing, we call the leftover ones "gizzards." They are little strips of fabric about 1/4 in. (6 mm) wide and can be cut with scissors, a rotary cutter, or a fabric cutter such as the Bee Line Cutter. This rug may have a funny name, but you'll have a great time knitting it up and enjoying it in your home.

■ NOTE

When you are working on the wrong side of this rug, the knots will automatically end up on the right side. When you are working on the right side, you will have to bring them from the wrong side to the right after completing the row, pulling them through either by hand or with a crochet hook.

■ PATTERN

Using a long-tail cast-on, CO 60 sts.

Row 1: Knit.

Row 2: Sl 1 pwise, k to end.

Repeat row 2 until the rug measures 30 inches or desired length.

BO loosely.

BORDERS

A border can be a way to snazz things up in a rug made from a plain color like black. It's also a great way to pick up on colors in a room.

A scrappy border made from various colors of yarn and fabric would look great on this rug. Knit small squares or rectangles approximately the width you want the border to be. They can be as long as you like. I used squares and rectangles that were approximately 3 by 3 in. (7.5 by 7.5 cm) or 3 by 5 in. (7.5 by 12.5 cm). When you have a few blocks completed, lay them along the side of the knitted rug to try out different orders and arrangements. When you have decided on an arrangement, pin the edges of the border pieces together with safety pins and sew them together with sewing thread. You can also crochet the pieces together with slip stitch or single crochet. Sew the border to the rug using sewing thread.

Variation

SAMPLE KNITTED BY JOAN MALLUM

The look of this rug can change quite a bit depending on the wool fabric you use for it. This one was made with a beautiful plaid fabric. The strips of wool used were all 9 in. (23 cm) long, unlike in the black rug, which used strips of wool in varying lengths. Using strips of the same length throughout the rug created a more even shag effect.

There are other possibilities for variations on this rug. You can use all different colors randomly chosen for a hit-or-miss rug. You could also use three different values (light, medium, and dark) of one color; if you used just two colors you could alternate them. You could tie the strips on as you knit, using just one color per row, with several rows of one color, then a wide stripe of another color. So many possibilities!

■ Feelin' Groovy T-Shirt Rug

MATERIALS
About 8 white T-shirts without side seams
Rit dye Bright Pack (contains yellow, green, blue, and red dyes)

NEEDLES
U.S. size 17 (12.75 mm) 24-inch circular needles

GAUGE
2.5 sts = 1 in. (2.5 cm) in garter stitch

FINISHED MEASUREMENTS
24 by 18 in. (61 by 46 cm)

■ PREPARING THE T-SHIRTS

Lay out a shirt flat and cut off the bottom hem. Starting anywhere on the bottom edge, cut up into the shirt on a gentle diagonal until you have a strip 1 in. (2.5 cm) wide. Continue cutting around and around the T-shirt in a spiral, keeping the strip a constant width. When you get to the arms, taper the strip off to a point.

Pull on the T-shirt strip to stretch it out, then roll into a ball.

Repeat with the other shirts.

Our example took about 8 large shirts, but this can vary, depending on the size of the shirts and what size rug you want to make.

■ DYEING INSTRUCTIONS

1. Cut the T-shirt strips into 18-in. (46 cm) lengths, leaving two 12-yard strips to use for the beginning and end of the rug. Tie the strips together in bundles.

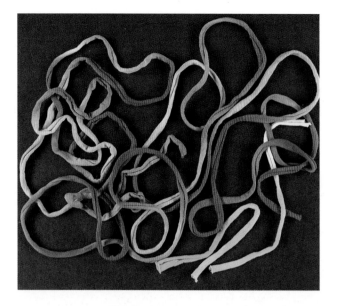

2. Soak the bundles of strips in water. Wring out and lay on plastic wrap.

3. Mix together about ⅛ cup Rit dye with ⅛ cup hot water and 1 teaspoon salt in a squirt bottle. Shake to mix, covering the opening with a gloved hand.

4. Squirt the dye onto the bundles of strips, starting with yellow, then moving on to green, blue, and finally red. Make sure dye goes in between individual strips. Try slightly overlapping the colors, or leave white space between colors if desired.

5. Close the plastic wrap around the dyed T-shirt strips. If needed, add more plastic wrap to make sure strips are completely covered on all sides and ends.

6. Microwave for 2 minutes on high. Let cool.

7. Rinse the strips thoroughly with cold water. Dry in dryer.

▓ PATTERN

With one of the 12-yard pieces of T-shirt yarn, CO 50 sts using a long-tail cast-on.

Rows 1–2: Knit.

Join the 18-in. (46 cm) lengths of T-shirt together with overhand knots, leaving 2-in. (5 cm) tails on each knot. This will create your shag effect. Break off the original yarn (if any remains from the original 12-yard piece) and join the knotted yarn.

Row 3 (RS): Sl 1 pwise, k to end.

Row 4 (WS): Sl 1 pwise, k to end.

Repeat Rows 3–4 until piece measures 30 in. (76 cm) or desired length. Break off the knotted yarn and join the remaining long piece of yarn. Knit 2 rows even. Bind off.

Weave in ends.

▓ NOTE

When you are working on the wrong side, the knots will automatically end up on the right side of the work. When you are working on the right side, the knots will end up on the wrong side and you will have to pull them through to the right side after completing the row—either by hand or with a crochet hook.

■ Mad About Plaid

MATERIALS
About 6 wool Pendleton shirts
About 1 yd. of wool fabric in a contrasting color or about 220 yd. (200 m) of worsted-weight yarn

NEEDLES
U.S. size 11 (8 mm) 10-inch straight needles

NOTIONS
Large tapestry needle
Stitch markers or safety pins

GAUGE
3 sts = 1 in. (2.5 cm) in garter stitch

FINISHED MEASUREMENTS
40 in. (102 cm) in diameter

This rug is a variation on a traditional knitted rug from the murky mists of our Americana fiber arts past. Our resourceful ancestors would make their rugs out of any unneeded materials on hand. Once plaid wool shirts had outlived their usefulness as garments, the fabric would be cut into strips and knit into a cozy rug for a drafty farm house or cabin. Can't you just imagine Auntie Em having one in her humble home before the twister swooped Dorothy off to Oz?

■ NOTE

Always slip the first stitch purlwise on even rows. This will create a natural curve, making sewing the rug together easier. Be careful not to allow the rug to "cup" when you sew it together.

■ PREPARING THE SHIRTS

Using sharp scissors, cut the collar and arms from the body of the shirt. Cut open the arms on one side of the seam, then cut off the seam and the cuffs. Cut the back from the shirt, cutting right along the seams. Cut the button bands and side seams off the front of the shirt. Finally, remove the pockets by cutting close around them.

To turn the shirt fabric into yarn, cut the fabric pieces into rectangles (they will vary in size depending on where they came from on the shirt). Fold each rectangle in half. Using a rotary cutter or sharp scissors, make a cut parallel to the edge of the piece, about ¼ in. (6 mm) from the edge, from the folded edge to within ⅜ in. (1 cm) from the top. Repeat across the piece, making all the cuts ¼ in. (6 mm) apart, until you reach the other edge of the rectangle. Open up the fabric and lay it flat. Using scissors, finish cutting the last ⅜ inch of the first cut on the top edge of the piece only. Skip the next cut, and finish the one after that. Continue to finish cutting the last ⅜ in. (1 cm) of every other cut all the way across the fabric along the top edge.

Repeat on the bottom edge of the piece, making sure to finish only the cuts that you skipped on the top edge. You should end up with the entire rectangle cut into a zigzag piece of fabric. Roll this strip of fabric into a ball.

Do the same with the other rectangles, sewing the strips together with matching thread each time you add a new one to the ball. Prepare the other shirts in the same way. If using wool fabric to assemble the rug, cut it into strips as well.

You can also use a fabric cutter such as the Bee Line cutter to cut the fabric into strips.

■ NOTE

When knitting this rug, you can change color as often as you like, or you can just knit with one plaid until it runs out and then change to a new one.

■ PATTERN

CO 2 sts.
Row 1: K2.
Row 2: Sl 1, k1.

Rows 3–12: Repeat rows 1–2.
Row 13: K1, M1, k1. (3 sts)
Row 14: Sl 1, k2.
Row 15: K3.
Rows 16–18: Repeat rows 14–15, ending with a repeat of row 14.
Row 19: K1, M1, k2. (4 sts)
Row 20: Sl 1, k3.
Row 21: K4.
Rows 22–26: Repeat rows 20–21, ending with a repeat of row 20.
Row 27: K1, M1, k3. (5 sts)
Row 28: Sl 1, k4.
Row 29: K5.
Row 30–40: Repeat rows 28–29, ending with a repeat of row 28.
Row 41: K1, M1, k4. (6 sts)
Row 42: Sl 1, k5.
Row 43: K6.
Rows 44–58: Repeat rows 42–43, ending with a repeat of row 42.
Row 59: K1, M1, k5. (7 sts)
Row 60: Sl 1, k6.
Row 61: K7.
Rows 62–82: Repeat rows 60–61, ending with a repeat of row 60.
Row 83: K1, M1, k6. (8 sts)
Row 84: Sl 1, k7.
Row 85: K8.
Repeat rows 84–85 until rug is the desired size, ending with a repeat of row 84.

Put sts on a holder. Coil rug into a spiral and whipstitch together with strips of wool fabric or with two strands of worsted-weight yarn held together, starting in the middle.

You can also sew the rug together a little bit at a time rather than knitting the majority of it before sewing. This allows you to make choices on color placement and gives you a better idea of the size of your rug. As the size increases, it may be helpful to place the rug on a table while knitting.

Place 6 stitch markers or safety pins evenly spaced along the outside edge of the assembled rug. These indicate when to work decrease rows.

Put live stitches back on needles.
Next row (odd): Knit.
Next row (even): Sl 1, k7.

Repeat these 2 rows around the rug, substituting one of the following decrease rows for the odd row every time you reach one of your 6 markers—decrease row 1 when you reach the first marker, decrease row 2 when you reach the second marker, and so on.

Decrease Row 1: K3, k2tog, k3. (7 sts)
Decrease Row 2: K2, k2tog, k3. (6 sts)
Decrease Row 3: K2, k2tog, k2. (5 sts)
Decrease Row 4: K1, k2tog, k2. (4 sts)
Decrease Row 5: K1, k2tog, k1. (3 sts)
Decrease Row 6: K2tog, k1. (2 sts)

After working decrease row 6, k2tog. Cut wool "yarn" and pull end through last st.

FINISHING

Weave in ends. Whipstitch the decrease round to the rest of the rug.

TIP

For an extra finish, crochet around the edge of the rug with the same material you used to sew the strip together.

Denim Fluff Rug

SAMPLE KNITTED BY BRADLEY DUCK

YARN

4 Medium Coats Creme de la Crème (100% combed cotton; 126 yd./115 m; 2 oz./71 g), 2 skeins Ecru Fleck

NEEDLES

U.S. size 8 (5 mm) 24-inch circular needles

OTHER MATERIALS

Old denim blue jeans (our rug used about 6 pairs of women's size medium jeans)

GAUGE

9 sts = 1 in. (2.5 cm) in garter stitch

FINISHED MEASUREMENTS

24 in. (61 cm) square

How could I turn down the offer of a dozen boxes of worn blue jeans? My husband was not so thrilled when I brought home the boxes, trying to sell him on all of the wonderful projects that I would create from those fashion staples.

I won't confess to how many years ago that was, but I have slowly made a small dent in my denim supply. This rug was inspired by the need to find another use for all of those blue jeans with a nod to our industrious ancestors who never let anything go to waste. Based on a traditional Americana rug, this twenty-first-century version gives you a way to repurpose those pairs of worn-out jeans.

◼ PREPARING THE FABRIC

Cut the jeans in ½ by 4 in. (1.2 by 10 cm) strips. Try using a variety of darker and lighter denim mixed together. To get an even distribution of lights and darks, put your strips in a bag and toss them like a salad. Randomly grab strips as you knit.

◼ PATTERN

CO 54 stitches.

Row 1: Knit.

Row 2: *Insert needle into next stitch. Fold a piece of denim in half over the working yarn. Knit the stitch tightly. The denim will be caught in the stitch as it is knit. Repeat from * all the way across the row. **Note:** *Be sure to pull extra tight when knitting a piece of denim into the rug.*

Repeat rows 1 and 2 until the rug measures approximately 28 inches or desired length.

Knit 2 rows even, without strips.

BO.

FINISHING

Weave in yarn ends.

W hat is there not to like about stripes? I love horizontal, vertical, and even diagonal stripes. Stripes are wonderful wide and certainly nice narrow. And of course, I love mixing it all up with wide and narrow stripes together. Did I neglect to mention all of the different color combinations with stripes? Do wavy and zigzag stripes count too? I think so. The possibilities are endless!

Rather than playing it straight with our stripes, we went zigzaggy, wavy, and diagonal for a collection of subtle to bold rugs for your home in color combinations to please every knitter.

Diagonal Stripes Rug

YARN

Cascade 128 (100% super-wash merino wool, 128 yd./117 m; 3.5 oz./100 g)

- **3 skeins Color A:** Granny Smith (8914)
- **1 skein Color B:** Fall Foliage (9581)
- **1 skein Color C:** Cordovan (9408)

NEEDLES

U.S. size 7 (4.5 mm) 36-inch circular needles

GAUGE

5 sts = 1 in. (2.5 cm) in garter stitch

FINISHED MEASUREMENTS

30 by 20 in. (76 by 51 cm), without fringe

There are lots of happy accidents in any creative pursuit. Making something can be like taking a journey to one place, but deciding along the way to go somewhere else instead. That certainly was true in creating this rug. After the sample knitter finished the knitting, we didn't have the heart to ask her to work in all of those ends—a job no knitter likes. After much discussion, it was decided that the rug would look fantastic if we just left the ends as a fringe. All that was needed was to add more fringe to the bottom and side edges. Who says fringe has to be symmetrically placed? A side benefit of the fringe is that it makes this rug reversible. The jury is still out as to which side is the best. You will have to decide that for yourself by knitting this beauty and trying it out, flipping it over every other day.

■ NOTE

When changing color, always leave at least a 4 in. (10 cm) or longer tail. This will later be incorporated into the fringe.

■ PATTERN

With color A, CO 2 sts.
Row 1: K1, kfb. (3 sts)
Row 2: K1, kfb, k1. (4 sts)
Row 3: K to last 2 sts, kfb, k1.
Rows 4–6: Repeat row 3.
Break off color A, leaving a 4 in. (10 cm) tail, and join color B.
Rows 7–12: Repeat row 3.
Break off color B and join color A.
Rows 13–18: Repeat row 3.
Break off color A and join color C.
Rows 19–24: Repeat row 3.
Break off color C and join color A.
Rows 25–30: Repeat row 3.
Break off color A and join color B.
Rows 31–120: Repeat rows 7–30, ending with a repeat of row 24 (after the 5th repeat of color C). You should have 20 diagonal stripes at this point.
Break off color C and join color A.
Row 121: K to last 2 sts, kfb, k1.
Row 122: K to last 3 sts, k2tog, k1.
Rows 123–126: Repeat rows 121–122.
Break off color A and join color B.
Rows 127–132: Repeat rows 121–122.
Break off color B and join color A.
Rows 133–138: Repeat rows 121–122.
Break off color A and join color C.
Rows 139–144: Repeat rows 121–122.

Break off color C and join color A.
Rows 145–192: Repeat rows 121–144.
You should have 8 repeats of the color sequence in all at this point (32 stripes).
Row 193: K to last 3 sts, k2tog, k1.
Rows 194–198: Repeat row 193.
Break off color A and join color B.
Rows 199–204: Repeat row 193.
Break off color B and join color A.
Rows 205–210: Repeat row 193.
Break off color A and join color C.
Rows 211–216: Repeat row 193.
Break off color C and join color A.
Rows 217–311: Repeat rows 193–216.
Row 312: K3tog.
Break yarn and pull tail through remaining stitch to fasten off.

FINISHING

You will have fringe on two adjacent sides of the rug. Make more fringe from each color of yarn by wrapping the yarn several times around a piece of cardboard about $4^1/2$ in. (11 cm) wide and cutting along one edge of the cardboard. This will give you 9-inch strands of fringe.

To add fringe to the rug, fold a strand of fringe in half. Insert a crochet hook through the rug right along the edge, and use it to pull the folded end of the fringe through. Bring the loose ends of the fringe up and pull them through the loop formed. Pull tight.

Add three strands of fringe to each stripe (in addition to the tails left over from knitting the rug) along both edges with tails, leaving the other two edges without fringe.

Lay the rug on a cutting mat and use a rotary cutter to trim the fringe to 3 in. (8 cm) or desired length.

Picasso Harlequin Rug

YARN

5 Bulky Cascade 128 (100% superwash merino wool, 128 yd./117 m; 3.5 oz./100 g)

- **4 skeins Color A:** Black (8555)
- **3 skeins Color B:** Natural (8010)

NEEDLES

U.S. size 7 (4.5 mm) 36-inch circular needles
U.S. size 7 (4.5 mm) double-pointed needles

OTHER MATERIALS

ProChem Yellow 119, Blue 490, and Magenta 338 dyes

NOTIONS

5 stitch holders (or pieces of scrap yarn)
13 bobbins (see tip below for an alternative to bobbins)

GAUGE

5 sts = 1 in. (2.5 cm) in garter stitch

FINISHED MEASUREMENTS

36 by 20 in. (91 by 51 cm)

The Harlequin, a stock character in Italian comedies of the seventeenth century, was a sort of trickster or clown character. His characteristic checkered costume is shown in a variety of colors, but the most memorable version is in striking black and white. Pablo Picasso was among a number of artists fascinated by this masked figure in diamond-patterned tights. With Picasso's paintings as an inspiration, we decided to bring it up a notch and add just a hint of color in the white portion of this rug to make it as playful as the comedic figure.

■ NOTE

This rug is worked in intarsia. Make sure to twist the yarn when changing colors, by bringing the color about to be knit under and to the right of the color just used.

TIP

Rather than using bobbins, you can use plastic baggies. Divide each skein of yarn into two balls and place each in a baggie. Line up baggies with Color A on one side of a shoebox and Color B on the other so that you can move the balls, untwisting them as you work. When you complete a row of knitting, lay your work on top of the shoebox and turn the box around. Flip the work over toward you and start the next row. This will help prevent tangles.

◼ DYEING INSTRUCTIONS

1. Wind the natural yarn into loose skeins to prevent tangles. Soak in cool water.
2. Prepare the yellow, blue, and magenta dyes separately, mixing $1/128$ teaspoon of each dye with 2 cups of water.
3. Place a piece of fabric in the bottom of an oven-proof pan (to absorb excess dye), then place the yarn on top.
4. Pour dye onto yarn in spots. Cover with a solution of 2 cups water to 1 teaspoon citric acid.
5. Cover pan with aluminum foil and bake at 350 degrees for 1 hour or until all dye has been absorbed. Let cool.
6. Wash yarn with a couple drops of detergent (put yarn in a zippered bag if using a washing machine) to remove the citric acid. Hang yarn to dry.

Wind seven bobbins with color A and six with color B.

◼ PATTERN

Using color A, CO 2 sts.
Rows 1–4: Knit.
Row 5: Kfb twice. (4 sts)
Rows 6–8: Knit.
Row 9: K1, kfb twice, k1. (6 sts)
Rows 10–12: Knit.
Row 13: K1, kfb, k2, kfb, k1. (8 sts)
Rows 14–16: Knit.
Row 17: K1, kfb, k4, kfb, k. (10 sts)
Rows 18–20: Knit.
Row 21: K1, kfb, k6, kfb, k1. (12 sts)
Rows 22–24: Knit.
Place live sts on a stitch holder or piece of scrap yarn.
Repeat six times, making a total of seven triangles in color A using a separate bobbin for each triangle.
Row 25: Put the first triangle onto circular needles and knit across as follows: *K1, kfb, k8, kfb, k1. (14 sts)

Using a bobbin of color B and double-pointed needles, CO 2 sts. Put onto circular needles. Place sts of another triangle of A on circular needles. Repeat from * five more times. Take up last triangle and knit across as for the others.
Rows 26–28: Knit, working each stitch in the established color.
Row 29: *With A, k1, k2tog, k8, k2tog, k1; with B, kfb twice. Repeat from * five more times. With A, k1, k2tog, k8, k2tog, k1.
Rows 30–32: Knit.
Row 33: *With A, k1, k2tog, k6, k2tog, k1; with B, k1, kfb twice, k1. Repeat from * five more times. With A, k1, k2tog, k6, k2tog, k1.
Rows 34–36: Knit.
Row 37: *With A, k1, k2tog, k4, k2tog, k1; with B, k1, kfb, k2, kfb, k1. Repeat from * five more times. With A, k1, k2tog, k4, k2tog, k1.
Rows 38–40: Knit.
Row 41: *With A, k1, k2tog, k2, k2tog, k1; with B, k1, kfb, k4, kfb, k1. Repeat from * five more times. With A, k1, k2tog, k2, k2tog, k1.
Rows 42–44: Knit.
Row 45: *With A, k1, k2tog twice, k1; with B, k1, kfb, k6, kfb, k1. Repeat from * five more times. With A, k1, k2tog twice, k1.
Rows 46–48: Knit.
Row 49: *With A, k2tog twice; with B, k1, kfb, k8, kfb, k1. Repeat from * five more times. With A, k2tog twice.
Rows 50–52: Knit.
Row 53: *With A, kfb twice; with B, k1, k2tog, k8, k2tog, k1. Repeat from * five more times. With A, kfb twice.
Rows 54–56: Knit.
Row 57: *With A, k1, kfb twice, k1; with B, k1, k2tog, k6, k2tog, k1. Repeat from * five more times. With A, k1, kfb twice, k1.
Rows 58–60: Knit.
Row 61: *With A, k1, kfb, k2, kfb, k1; with B, k1, k2tog, k4, k2tog, k1. Repeat from * five more times. With A, k1, kfb, k2, kfb, k1.
Rows 62–64: Knit.
Row 65: *With A, k1, kfb, k4, kfb, k1; with B, k1, k2tog, k2, k2tog, k1. Repeat from * five more times. With A, k1, kfb, k4, kfb, k1.
Rows 66–68: Knit.
Row 69: *With A, k1, kfb, k6, kfb, k1; with B, k1, k2tog twice, k1. Repeat from * five more times. With A, k1, kfb, k6, kfb, k1.
Rows 70–72: Knit.

Row 73: *With A, k1, kfb, k8, kfb, k1; with B, k2tog twice. Repeat from * five more times. With A, k1, kfb, k8, kfb, k1.

Rows 74–76: Knit.

Rows 77–268: Repeat rows 29–76 four more times.

Rows 269–315: Repeat rows 29–75.

Row 316: *With A, k14; with B, bind off next 2 sts. Repeat from * five more times. With A, k14.

You will now knit the end of each diamond separately to complete this end of the rug.

Working only on one diamond with A, work as follows:

Row 1: K1, k2tog, k8, k2tog, k1.

Rows 2–4: Knit.

Row 5: K1, k2tog, k6, k2tog, k1.

Rows 6–8: Knit.

Row 9: K1, k2tog, k4, k2tog, k1.

Rows 10–12: Knit.

Row 13: K1, k2tog, k2, k2tog, k1.

Rows 14–16: Knit.

Row 17: K1, k2tog twice, k1.

Rows 18–20: Knit.

Row 21: K2tog twice.

Rows 22–23: Knit.

Bind off.

Repeat for the other remaining diamonds.

FINISHING

Weave in ends.

Lava Lamp Rug

YARN

Cascade 220 (100% wool; 220 yd./200 m; 3.5 oz/100g), 1 skein each of the following colors:

- **Color A:** Celery (9407)
- **Color B:** Dusty Rose (8114)
- **Color C:** Spring Meadow (2438)
- **Color D:** Mauve Heather (9441)
- **Color E:** Pear (8412)
- **Color F:** Light Purple (8420)
- **Color G:** Gold (9463B)
- **Color H:** Mystic Purple (2450)
- **Color I:** Mimosa (2436)
- **Color J:** Montmartre (2423)
- **Color K:** Nectarine (2451)
- **Color L:** Sapphire Heather (9456)
- **Color M:** Baby Rose Heather (9442)

NEEDLES

U.S. size 7 (4.5 mm) 36-inch circular needles

FINISHED MEASUREMENTS

36 by 32 in. (91 by 81 cm)

Lava or astro lamps were invented by British accountant Edward Craven-Walker. Who says accountants aren't a fun lot? He was inspired by a homemade egg timer bubbling on his local pub's stove top. The waxy blobs in these colorful lamps resemble pahoehoe lava, thus the name lava lamp.

Either you're old enough to remember when the lava lamp first hit the scene and was the must-have accessory for every dorm room from coast to coast—or you are young enough to remember its return in the late 1990s. Either way, get ready to plug in and knit by the light of your lava lamp.

■ NOTES

1. Hold two strands of yarn together throughout the rug.
2. Make sure to twist the yarns when you change from one color to another. The yarn just knit with will go to the left and over the new yarn.

■ PATTERN

Using a long-tail cast-on, CO as follows: 6 sts with color A, 16 sts with color B, 6 sts with color C, 16 sts with color D, 6 sts with color E, 16 sts with color F, 6 sts with color G, 16 sts with color H, 6 sts with color I, 16 sts with color J, 6 sts with color K, 16 sts with color L, 6 sts with color M.

Rows 1–2: Work even in garter stitch, working each stitch in the same color as in the previous row.

Row 3: *K1, M1R, k4, M1L, k1, change to next color, k1, ssk, k10, k2tog, k1, change to next color; repeat from * five more times, k1, M1R, k4, M1L, k1.

Row 4 and all even rows unless otherwise indicated: Purl, working each stitch in the same color as in the previous row.

Row 5: *K1, M1R, k6, M1L, k1, change to next color, k1, ssk, k8, k2tog, k1, change to next color; repeat from * five more times, k1, M1R, k6, M1L, k1.

Row 7: *K1, M1R, k8, M1L, k1, change to next color, k1, ssk, k6, k2tog, k1, change to next color; repeat from * five more times, k1, M1R, k8, M1L, k1.

Row 9: *K1, M1R, k10, M1L, k1, change to next color, k1, ssk, k4, k2tog, k1, change to next color; repeat from * five more times, k1, M1R, k10, M1L, k1.

Row 11: *K1, M1R, k12, M1L, k1, change to next color, k1, ssk, k2, k2tog, k1, change to next color; repeat from * five more times, k1, M1R, k12, M1L, k1.

Row 13: *K1, ssk, k10, k2tog, k1, change to next color, k1, M1R, k4, M1L, k1, change to next color; repeat from * five more times, k1, ssk, k10, k2tog, k1.

Row 15: *K1, ssk, k8, k2tog, k1, change to next color, k1, M1R, k6, M1L, k1, change to next color; repeat from * five more times, k1, ssk, k8, k2tog, k1.

Row 17: *K1, ssk, k6, k2tog, k1, change to next color, k1, M1R, k8, M1L, k1, change to next color; repeat from * five more times, k1, ssk, k6, k2tog, k1.

Row 19: *K1, ssk, k4, k2tog, k1, change to next color, k1, M1R, k10, M1L, k1, change to next color; repeat from * five more times, k1, ssk, k4, k2tog, k1.

Row 21: *K1, ssk, k2, k2tog, k1, change to next color, k1, M1R, k12, M1L, k1, change to next color; repeat from * five more times, k1, ssk, k2, k2tog, k1.

Repeat Rows 3–22 eight more times for a square rug, or thirteen more times for a rectangular rug.

Knit two rows even, working each stitch in the same color as in the previous row.

BO.

FINISHING

Weave in ends.

Zigzag Rug

YARN

4 Medium Cascade 220 (100% wool; 220 yd./200 m; 3.5 oz/100g):

- **5 skeins color A:** Pacific (2433)
- **1 skein Cherry** (2426)
- **1 skein Flamingo Pink** (7805)
- **1 skein Christmas Red Heather** (9488)
- **1 skein Cerise** (7802)

Hold Cherry and Flamingo Pink together for color B, and Christmas Red Heather and Cerise together for color C.

NEEDLES

U.S. size 9 (5.5 mm) 36-inch circular needles

NOTIONS

6 stitch markers

GAUGE

4 sts = 1 in. (4 cm) in garter stitch

FINISHED MEASUREMENTS

27 by 19 in. (69 by 48 cm)

What do lightning, electrical hazards, pinking shears, ravioli pasta, bargello, and the flag of Nagorono-Karabakh have in common? Zigzags! What is there not to love about a zigzag pattern? With our rug we upped the fun factor with great bright colors—pinky corals peeking through turquoise zigs (or is it zags?). You too will have fun as you zigzag your way through this rug. By the way, Nagorono-Karabakh is not yet an official country, but they have their zigzag flag ready to go if and when that happens.

■ NOTE

Hold two strands of yarn together throughout the rug. Colors B and C are each comprised of two different colors.

■ PATTERN

Holding two strands of color A together, CO 98 sts, placing a marker after every 14 sts.

SETUP ROWS:

Setup Row 1 (WS): Knit.
Setup Row 2 (RS): *K2tog, k4, kfb twice, k4, ssk; repeat from * across.
Setup Row 3: Repeat setup row 1.
Setup Row 4: Repeat setup row 2.
Break color A; join color C.
Setup Row 5: Repeat setup row 1.

PATTERN ROWS

Row 1 (RS): *K2tog, k4, kfb twice, k4, ssk; rep from * across.

Row 2 (WS): Purl.
Row 3: Repeat row 1.
Row 4: Repeat row 2.
Break color C; join color A.
Row 5: *K2tog, k4, kfb twice, k4, ssk; repeat from * across.
Row 6: Knit.
Row 7: Repeat row 5.
Row 8: Repeat row 6.
Row 9: Repeat row 5.
Row 10: Repeat row 6.
Break color A; join color B.
Rows 11–14: Repeat rows 1–4.
Break color B, join color A.
Rows 15–20: Repeat rows 5–10.
Break color A, join color C.
Repeat rows 1–20 seven more times. BO loosely.

FINISHING

Weave in ends.

I-CORD RUGS

The humble I-cord is simply a knitted tube, usually 4 stitches around and worked in a continuous spiral in the round. But despite its simplicity, it can make some very exciting and fun rugs.

The most time-consuming part of the process is making the I-cord itself. This can be done several different ways: The easiest is to use a knitting spool. People used to make these by driving nails into the top of a wooden spool; you can still do this today (or attach nails to a length of PVC pipe to accommodate bulkier yarns), but it is much simpler just to buy one of the ready-made knitting spools such as the Wonder Knitter.

You can also knit an I-cord on double-pointed needles, if you don't have a knitting spool. Cast on 4 stitches (or as many stitches as you want the I-cord to be around) and knit across them. When you get to the end, move the needle from your right hand to your left hand (or from left to right, for lefties) *without turning it*; slide the stitches down to the other end of the needle and pull the working yarn around, and begin knitting across in the same direction as before. (You are essentially knitting in the round, but on only 2 needles instead of 4.) This method is not as fast or easy as using a knitting spool, but it produces the same end result.

The Long Road Runner

MATERIALS
⅛ yard each of 29 different wool plaid fabrics
Red Heart Super Saver Yarn (100% acrylic, 160 yd./146 m; 3 oz./85 g), 1 skein black

TOOLS
Knitting spool

NOTIONS
Tapestry needle

FINISHED MEASUREMENTS
32 by 24 in. (81 by 61 cm)

I don't know what it is, but kids have always enjoyed the creative tedium of knitting spools—those little devices for making I-cords (you can buy one or make your own by hammering a few nails into the top of a large wooden spool). The Wonder Knitter is an updated and improved version of this old classic. But if you let your kids or grandkids see you making cord with your knitting spool, they're going to want in on the action. At this point, you have two choices. You can hand the making of the I-cords for this rug over to them or buy them knitting spools of their own to assist you in I-cord making. Either way, you win, creating both a rug and also good memories.

▨ PREPARING THE WOOL

Use a Bee Line fabric cutter, a rotary cutter and cutting mat, or scissors to cut the wool fabric into $\frac{3}{16}$ inch (5 mm) wide strips. As you knit, you will tie on new strips as needed.

▨ PATTERN

Using a knitting spool, knit a 1 yd. (0.9 m) long 6-stitch I-cord from each plaid. When changing from one strip of wool to another, tie with an overhand knot. As you knit, allow the knot to go to the inside of the cord. When you finish an I-cord, fasten it off by pulling the tail end through the 6 stitches. Pull the tails at both ends to the inside of the cord to hide them.

Arrange the I-cords and pin them together so that they won't shift. Sew the I-cords together two at a time with black yarn, sewing across them widthwise from one to the next, occasionally working a backstitch. Leave the first and last $2\frac{1}{4}$ in. (5.7 cm) unsewn for a fringe.

■ Word Rug

MATERIALS

Coat-weight wool fabric of the size you want the finished rug to be

4 Medium — Lion's Brand Vanna's Choice (100% acrylic; 3.5 oz./100 g; 170 yd./156 m), 1 skein Brick

6 Super Bulky — Lion's Brand Chenille (75% acrylic, 18% polyester, 7% nylon; 2.5 oz/70 g; 100 yd./91 m), 1 skein Brick

TOOLS

Knitting spool

NOTIONS

Size 5 perle cotton in same color as wool fabric
Thread to match all yarns
Pins
Sewing needle
White chalk

FINISHED MEASUREMENTS

27 by 18 in. (69 by 46 cm) oval

Imagine having company over and greeting them with a friendly "Hello"—on a rug you made. Of course, you don't need to stop there. How about a gift to a friend or family member with the word "Love"? Perhaps a wedding or baby gift in the form of a handmade monogrammed rug. You are only limited by your imagination!

■ PATTERN

The first step is to choose a word! Next, cut out two pieces of wool in the shape and size you want your rug to be. Draw the word on the right side of one of the pieces of wool with white chalk.

Using a knitting spool, knit I-cords for your word from worsted-weight yarn. In our example, we used three separate pieces for the H, but one continuous piece for the rest of the word. Keep checking the length of your I-cords as you knit them. You can check the I-cord against the rug each time, or lay a piece of yarn on top of your word, then cut it and use it as reference for the length of cord you need.

Pin the cords onto the wool base. Hand sew them in place with whipstitch, making sure to catch just the edge of each I-cord.

Make an I-cord for the edge of the rug from super bulky yarn. When you have some length on the cord, start pin-ning it to the edge and sewing it in place, making sure to catch just the center of the I-cord. Do not sew both sides down. Continue adding to the I-cord, pinning it down, and sewing onto the rug until you reach the beginning of the border.

Pin the front of the rug to the back and sew the two pieces together around the edge with perle cotton and but-tonhole stitch.

■ Huichol Yarn Painting Rug

SAMPLE KNITTED BY LESLIE ROGERS

YARN

Cascade 220 (100% wool; 220 yd./200 m; 3.5 oz/100g), 1 skein each of the following colors:

- ■ *Color A:* Black (8555)
- ■ *Color B:* Beige (8021)
- ■ *Color C:* Camel (8622)
- ■ *Color D:* Pacific (2433)

NEEDLES

U.S. size 6 (4 mm) double-pointed needles

OTHER MATERIALS

Coat-weight wool fabric, two 23 by 33 inch pieces
Six scrap pieces of plaid wool fabric, approximately 7 by 14 in. (18 by 36 cm)
#18 chenille needle
Sewing needle
Thread to match all yarns
4 skeins embroidery floss in any contrasting color

FINISHED MEASUREMENTS

33 by 24 in. (84 by 61 cm)

The Huichol people of Mexico create colorful yarn "paintings" using traditional patterns. Yarn is pressed into a wax-covered board to form a design spiraling from the outside of a shape to the inside, completely filling in the shape with fiber. Wales is a long way from Mexico and a Welsh Terrier is hardly a traditional Huichol pattern, but we decided to design a tribute to a certain author's pet. We think the terrier rug is so cute that you'll want one in your home. Maybe you'll even get the real thing to go along with your rug.

■ PATTERN

Place the terrier pattern (next page) on one piece of background wool. Using embroidery floss in a contrasting color, baste an outline around the terrier. This serves as a guide and will later be removed.

Cut out six diamonds from contrasting plaid wool and pin in place, referring to the photo. Sew the diamonds in place (this stitching will later be covered with an I-cord).

Using color B, start knitting a 4 stitch I-cord for the ear. Check to make sure you have enough to fill in the area before binding off and weaving in the ends. Sew the I-cord down on the background, working from the outside edge of the ear to the center in a spiral. Zigzag back and forth as you sew to catch both sides of the I-cord and make sure it is firmly sewed down.

Using color A, knit a short length of I-cord for the eye and another for the nose. Sew these down as before. Knit a longer I-cord for the "saddle" of the terrier with color A. Again, as for the ear, start by sewing it down around the outside edge and work in toward the center in a spiral.

Using color C, knit an I-cord for the body of the dog. Sew it down, working from the outside to the inside. You can work in a number of patterns—it will probably take a few different spirals to fill all parts of the dog.

Knit six lengths of I-cord in color D to outline the diamonds. Pin both ends of each I-cord to the bottom point of a diamond, then pin down the top point, and finally the side points. Sew the I-cords down as before.

Turn piece over and cut and remove the embroidery floss basting lines.

Place the undecorated piece of wool on a flat surface. Place the terrier piece on top, lining up the edges. Pin the two pieces together. With a chenille needle and two strands of turquoise yarn, blanket stitch around the outside edge.

If the rug is a little bit puckered, steam block it lightly so it will lie flat. To steam the rug, lay a damp towel on top of the rug and hold a steam iron about ½ in. (1.3 cm) above it. Do not rest the iron on the towel or rug. Or you can use a steamer that does not need to come in contact with the rug.

TIP

For this rug, it's a good idea to sew the I-cords down as you make them, or at least before you bind them off, to make sure you have the right length.

Updated Vintage I-Cord Rug

YARN

Medium

Red Heart Super Saver (100% acrylic; 160 yd./146 m; 3 oz./85 g), 1 skein each in black and various variegated colorways. Sample uses Bikini, Day Glow, Grape Fizz, Heartfelt, and Wildflower.

NEEDLES

U.S. size 7 (4.5 mm) double-pointed needles

NOTIONS

50 feet (15 m) ¼ in. (6 mm) nylon clothesline
Tapestry needle

FINISHED MEASUREMENTS

29 by 25 in. (74 by 64 cm) oval

The idea for this rug came from our vast collection of antique and vintage rugs. Whenever we come across a great find in an antique or junk shop, we always wonder who the creator of the rug was and where they used it. One of our finds was a coiled oval I-cord rug with alternating rounds of black and variegated yarns. We were inspired by the knitter's use of bright colors and the way the variegated yarns created wonderful and unexpected patterns when used in I-cords. We tried to do the same in our rug: We love bright colors, and decided not to hold back. And just like in the original, each brilliant variegated yarn revealed its own unique pattern. We did make one significant change—adding a nylon cord inside the I-cord for extra durability. Your own I-cord beauty will be a sturdy rug that can be handed down from one generation to the next instead of ending up in an anonymous junk shop, the way its ancestor did.

■ PATTERN

With black, CO 5 stitches. Knit one inch of I-cord. Insert clothesline into I-cord. Continue knitting I-cord around the clothesline until knitting measures 10 inches. This will be the center line of the oval rug. Break off the black yarn and join the variegated yarn and knit until the variegated section is long enough to wrap around the black center (about 22 inches). Coiling in a clockwise direction, sew the variegated section to the black center with black yarn. The variegated section should end just to the right of the top of the center. Break off the variegated yarn and rejoin black. Knit until the black section will go around the rug twice. Sew to the center section. Continue alternating between black and variegated yarn until rug measures about 20 by 30 inches, finishing with a black stripe. Make sure to always end the stripes in the same place. When the rug is just about completed, cut the nylon clothesline off at an angle. Continue to knit for about an inch past the end of the clothesline. Break the yarn, thread the tail through the live stitches, and pull tight. Sew the end down to the outer edge of the rug. Weave in ends.

TIP

When adding a new color, carry the tail of that new color inside the I-cord for about an inch before switching to that color.

TIP

When sewing the rug together, work on a flat surface such as a table. As the rug gets larger, it may be easier to knit with the rug on the table for extra support.

SPECIAL RUGS THAT DEFY CATEGORIES

This chapter could have been titled "miscellaneous," but somehow that just didn't seem to appropriately describe these rugs. We think all of the rugs in this book are wonderful (yes, we might be a little biased), but we do have a special spot in our hearts for the rugs in this chapter.

In this chapter, you will find weaving, dancing couples, and a rug that gives you a bird's-eye view of the earth. One rug invites you to take a walk along a sparsely traveled path through a forest of autumn colors with a splash of blue sky peeking through the trees. And oh how your feet will love the foot massage you'll get every time you walk across the ruching in the Good on the Feet Gathered Rug! Flip through the pages and you'll see why this collection of rugs defies being categorized. Their uniqueness will only add to the pleasure of making them and enjoying them in your home.

Woven Puzzle Rug

SAMPLE KNITTED BY SANDY TEBBS

YARN

Cascade 220 (100% wool; 220 yd./200 m; 3.5 oz/100g), 4 skeins each of the following colors:

- **Color A:** Lake Chelan Heather (9451)
- **Color B:** Aporto (4009)

NEEDLES

U.S. size 9 (5.5 mm) 36-inch circular needles

U.S. size 9 (5.5 mm) straight or double-pointed needles

NOTIONS

10 stitch holders (or pieces of scrap yarn)

GAUGE

4 sts = 1 in. (2.5 cm) in stockinette stitch

FINISHED MEASUREMENTS

25 in. (64 cm) square

As a child, I loved to weave pot holders. My mother had an endless supply, receiving them for her birthday, Christmas, and Mother's Day. This activity started a lifelong love of weaving in me. So why not combine knitting with weaving? That thought process was how this rug was born. This reversible rug is tremendously satisfying to knit, weave, and complete (although I must confess that until you get all the parts woven and sewn together, it can feel like knitting a giant octopus). Creating this rug is just as satisfying as making all those potholders for Mom.

■ NOTE

Hold two strands of yarn together throughout the rug.

■ PATTERN

FOUNDATION

CO 124 stitches with color A.

Row 1 (RS): *[K1, p2] 6 times, k3; repeat from * 5 times, [k1, p2] 6 times, k1.

Row 2 (WS): *[P1, k2] 6 times, p3; repeat from * 5 times, [p1, k2] 6 times, p1.

Rows 3–12: Repeat rows 1–2.

FIRST WEAVER

Row 1 (RS): [K1, p2] 6 times, ssk. (19 sts)

Put remaining sts on a stitch holder or a piece of scrap yarn.

Row 2 (WS): [P1, k2] 6 times, p1.

Row 3: [K1, p2] 6 times, k1.

Repeat rows 2–3 until the weaver measures 22 inches, not including the 12 rows at the beginning. Break yarn. Put stitches on a holder.

MIDDLE WEAVERS

Transfer next 21 sts from holder or scrap yarn to the needle and join yarn.

Row 1 (RS): K2tog, p2, [k1, p2] 5 times, ssk. (19 sts)

Row 2 (WS): [P1, k2] 6 times, p1.

Row 3: [K1, p2] 6 times, k1.

Repeat rows 2–3 until the weaver measures 22 inches, not including the 12 rows at the beginning. Break yarn. Put stitches on a holder.

Repeat 3 more times.

LAST WEAVER

Row 1 (RS): Ssk, [p2, k1] 6 times. (19 sts)

Row 2 (WS): P1, [k2, p1] 6 times.

Row 3: [K1, p2] 6 times, k1.

Repeat rows 2–3 until the weaver measures 22 inches, not including the 12 rows at the beginning. Break yarn.

ENDING

Put all weavers back on the circular needles in order. With RS facing, join yarn at the right-hand side and work across the entire row as follows:

Row 1 (RS): *[K1, p2] 6 times, kfbf (2 sts increased); repeat from * 4 more times, k1, [p2, k1] 6 times. (124 sts)

Row 2 (WS): *[P1, k2] 6 times, p4; repeat from * 4 more times, [k2, p1] 6 times.

Row 3: *[K1, p2] 6 times, k4; repeat from * 4 more times, [p2, k1] 6 times.

Rows 4–12: Repeat rows 2–3, ending with a row 2. BO in pattern.

SECOND PIECE

Repeat the above instructions using color B. Stop after finishing the last weaver to weave the weavers over and under the weavers of the first piece before working the ending.

FINISHING

Sew the weavers together where they cross to help secure and stabilize them. Weave in ends.

People Mover

YARN

Cascade 128 (100% superwash merino wool, 128 yd./117 m; 3.5 oz./100 g)

■ *5 skeins Color A:* Fudge Brownie (9606)
■ *5 skeins Color B:* Ecru (8019)

The ecru yarn used in our sample was spot dyed (see dyeing instructions below).

NEEDLES

U.S. size 7 (4.5 mm) 36-inch circular needles

OTHER MATERIALS

Cushing's acid dyes: Mint Green, Peach, Pink, and Aqualon Yellow

GAUGE

5 sts = 1 in. (2.5 cm) in garter stitch

FINISHED MEASUREMENTS

48 by 24 in. (122 by 61 cm)

Some knitters are intimidated by colorwork because knitting with two colors at once in a row is too daunting. But with slipped stitch patterns like this one, you can produce impressive color patterns without having to work with more than one color at a time. In this rug, you alternate two rows of the dark color with two rows of the light color, and simply slip the stitches that you don't want to be in the color you're currently using. If you can do a knit stitch and slip a stitch, you can do colorwork!

■ DYEING INSTRUCTIONS

1. Wind yarn into a loose skein to prevent tangles. Soak in hot water.
2. Mix $\frac{1}{128}$ teaspoon each of Mint Green, Peach, Pink, and Aqualon Yellow with 2 cups of boiling water in separate containers. Add 2 teaspoons of citric acid to each cup of dye solution.
3. Place a wet piece of wool fabric in the bottom of a flat ovenproof pan to absorb excess dye, then place the soaked yarn on top.
4. Pour spots of the various dyes onto yarn.
5. Cover the pan with foil and bake at 350 degrees for 1 hour. Let cool.
6. Wash yarn with a couple of drops of detergent to rinse out the citric acid. (If using a washing machine, put yarn in a zippered bag to prevent tangles.) Hang yarn to dry.

■ NOTE

Every time you change colors, twist the yarns together by bringing the new color under the old one and to the right.

■ PATTERN

With color A, CO 194 stitches.
Row 1: Knit.
Join color B (do not break color A).
Rows 2–3: With B, knit.
Rows 4–5: With A, knit.
Rows 6–7: With B, knit.
Rows 8–9: With A, knit, following the chart.
Rows 10–11: With B, knit, following the chart.
Rows 12–75: Follow rows 12–75 of the chart.

HOW TO READ A MOSAIC PATTERN CHART

Start the first row of the chart in the lower right-hand corner. Each row of the chart represents two rows of knitting, and the color being used for those rows is given in the box next to the row number. Knit the stitches shown in the color for the row and slip the others pwise wyib. On the next row, work exactly the same in reverse: If you knit a stitch on the first row, purl it on the return; if you slipped a stitch on the first row, slip it on the return with the yarn in front.

For example, rows 10 and 11 should be read as follows:

Row 10: With B, k3, *k1, sl 1, k1, sl 1 twice, k2, sl 1, k2, sl 1 twice, k1, sl 1 twice, k2, sl 1 twice, k1, sl 1; repeat from * to last 3 sts, k3.
Row 11: With B, p3, *sl 1, p1, sl 1 twice, p2, sl 1 twice, p1, sl 1 twice, p2, sl 1, p2, sl 1 twice, p1, sl 1, p1; repeat from * to last 3 sts, p3.

Rows 76–211: Repeat rows 8–75 of the chart two more times.
Rows 212–213: With A, knit.
Rows 214–215: With B, knit.
Row 216: With A, knit.
BO with A.

FINISHING

Weave in ends.

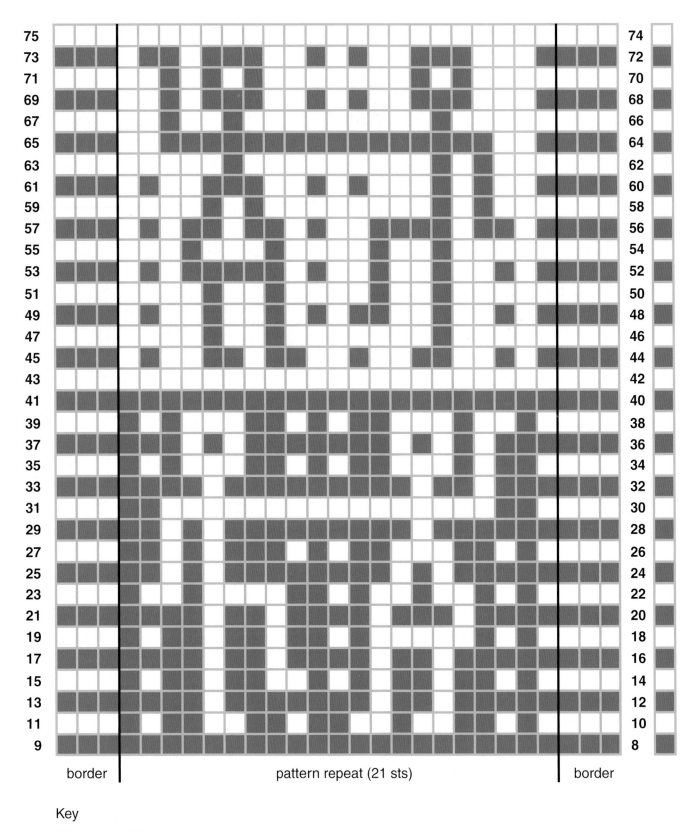

Key

□ white   ■ blue

■ All Squared Up

I once saw a painting that really struck me. Have you ever had the feeling you could walk right into a painting? That is how I felt about this one. It was a simple scene, just a path through the woods on a clear autumn day. The colors, all reds, golds, browns, and greens, were so compelling. What really called me into the painting was a little patch of blue sky at the end of the path. The startlingly warm colors of the trees were such a contrast to that little bit of azure. I wanted so badly to stroll down and see what was at the end of the overgrown road. The colors and subject of that painting were the inspiration for this rug. I tried to recreate the emotion I felt when first glancing at the painting with the warm colors of autumn surrounding a patch of blue in the center. Hopefully, that central square will draw you in as the painting did me.

■ PATTERN

Using color A and 52-inch circular needles, CO 384 stitches, placing a marker every 96 stitches. Join in round, being careful not to twist stitches.

Round 1: Purl.

Round 2: *K2tog, k to last 2 sts before marker, ssk; repeat from * around.

Rounds 3–7: Repeat rounds 1–2. (360 sts at end of round 7)

Break color A and join color B.

YARN

 Cascade 128 (100% superwash merino wool, 128 yd./117 m; 3.5 oz./100 g), 1 skein each of the following colors:

- ■ **Color A:** Van Dyke Brown (7822)
- ■ **Color B:** Walnut Heather (8013)
- ■ **Color C:** Cafe (2411)
- ■ **Color D:** Burnt Orange (9465B)
- ■ **Color E:** Rust (9581)
- ■ **Color F:** Doeskin Heather (8012)
- ■ **Color G:** Lichen (9338)
- ■ **Color H:** Straw (4010)
- ■ **Color I:** Ruby (9404)
- ■ **Color J:** Turtle (2452)
- ■ **Color K:** Summer Sky Heather (9452)

NEEDLES

U.S. size 8 (5 mm) 52-, 36-, 24-, and 16-inch circular needles

U.S. size 8 (5 mm) double-pointed needles

NOTIONS

4 stitch markers or safety pins

GAUGE

9 sts = 2 in. (5 cm) in garter stitch

FINISHED MEASUREMENTS

28 in. (71 cm) square

Round 8: *K2tog, k to last 2 sts before marker, ssk; repeat from * around.

Round 9: Knit.

Rounds 10–14: Repeat rounds 8–9. (328 sts at end of round 14)

Break color B and join color C. Change to 36-inch circular needle.

Round 15: Knit.

Round 16: *K2tog, k to last 2 sts before marker, ssk; repeat from * around.

Round 17: Purl.

Rounds 18–21: Repeat rounds 16–17. (304 sts at end of round 21)

Break color C and join color D.

Rounds 22–28: Repeat rounds 8–14. (272 sts at end of round 28)

Break color D and join color E.

Rounds 29–35: Repeat rounds 15–21. (248 sts at end of round 35)

Break color E and join color F.

Rounds 36–42: Repeat rounds 8–14. (216 sts at end of round 42)

Break color F and join color G.

Rounds 43–49: Repeat rounds 15–21. (192 sts at end of round 49)

Break color G and join color H.

Rounds 50–56: Repeat rounds 8–14. (160 sts at end of round 56)

Break color H and join color I. (160 sts)

Rounds 57–63: Repeat rounds 15–21. (136 sts at end of round 63)

Break color H and join color D. Change to 24-inch circular needle.

Rounds 64–70: Repeat rounds 8–14. (104 sts at end of round 70)

Break color D and join color J.

Rounds 71–77: Repeat rounds 15–21. (80 sts at end of round 77)

Break color J and join color K. Change to 16-inch circular needles.

Round 78: *K2tog, k to last 2 sts before marker, ssk; repeat from * around.

Round 79: Knit.

Rounds 80–94: Repeat rounds 78–79, switching to double-pointed needles when working on circular needles becomes too difficult. (8 sts at end of round 94)

Break yarn and thread end through remaining sts, pulling tight to secure. Weave in ends.

Good on the Feet
Gathered Rug

YARN

 4 **Medium**

Cascade 220 (100% wool; 220 yd./200 m; 3.5 oz/100g):

- **4 skeins color A:** Heather Tweed (7806)
- **5 skeins color B:** Summer Sky Heather (9452)

NEEDLES

U.S. size 9 (5.5 mm) 36-inch circular needles

GAUGE

4 sts = 1 in. (2.5 cm) in garter stitch

FINISHED MEASUREMENTS

34 by 26 in. (86 by 66 cm)

Imagine coming home after a long day on your feet and having someone waiting to massage them. As much as I would like to, I can't promise that, but walking on this rug with its ruching will be almost as good as that massage.

■ NOTE

Hold two strands of yarn together throughout the rug.

■ PATTERN

CO 80 sts with Color A using a long-tail cast-on.
Rows 1–5: Knit.
Row 6 (WS): Kfb in every st across. (160 sts)

Drop color A and join color B.

Row 7: Knit.

Row 8: Purl.

Rows 9–12: Repeat rows 7–8.

Drop color B and pick up color A.

Row 13: K2tog across. (80 sts)

Rows 14–17: Knit.

Drop color A and pick up color B.

Repeat rows 6–17 seventeen more times or until rug measures desired length.

BO.

FINISHING

Weave in ends.

A River Runs Through It

YARN

4 Medium Cascade 220 (100% wool; 220 yd./200 m; 3.5 oz/100g):

- ■ *5 skeins color A:* Celtic Green (9410)
- ■ *3 skeins color B:* Lichen (9338)
- ■ *2 skeins color C:* Turquoise Heather (9455)

NEEDLES
U.S. size 9 (5.5 mm) 36-inch circular needles
U.S. size 7 (4.5 mm) straight or double-pointed needles

OTHER MATERIALS
150 yd. #4 Krenik Metallic Thread in Blue Star (094)
10 yd. #16 Krenik Metallic Thread in Blue Ice (1432)

NOTIONS
Size H-8 (5 mm) crochet hook (optional)

GAUGE
4 sts = 1 in. (2.5 cm) in stockinette stitch using size 9 needles

FINISHED MEASUREMENTS
36 by 26 in. (91 by 66 cm)

In days gone by, when I used to fly small airplanes, I loved looking down on trees that looked like green tufts of cotton with the glint of the sun on a silver ribbon of a meandering river. Those memories inspired this rug. Instead of trees, we have blades of grass, but it still gives a bird's eye view somewhat like being in that plane. One thing you can't experience from a high altitude is the feel of those knitted shoots on your feet. This rug would be great for a child's room where they could use the rug to launch their imaginations, creating adventures on it with small figurines.

93

Key

☐ k on RS; P on WS   ⊡ p on RS; k on WS   ◉ Work grass with color A

▨ One strand each of color A and color B held together

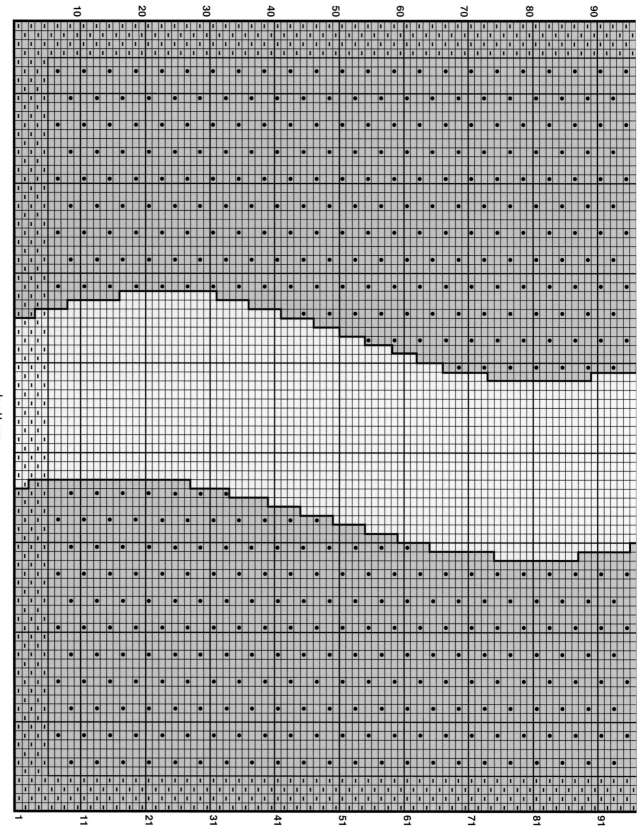

□ One strand color C and one strand metallic thread held together

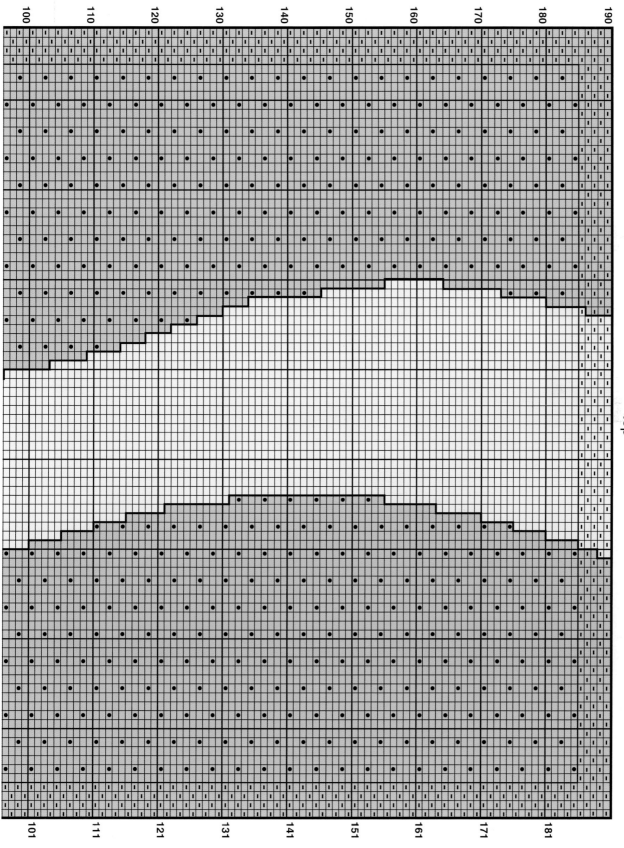

top

SPECIAL INSTRUCTIONS

Grass: To knit a blade of grass, knit the next stitch onto the smaller needle. Turn work. Using a knitted cast-on and only the lighter green strand of working yarn, CO 9 stitches. Bind off 9 stitches. Slip remaining stitch back onto larger needles and resume knitting across the row.

■ NOTES

1. Hold one strand each of the greens together throughout the green areas of the rug except when knitting a blade of grass. For the grass, use one strand of the lighter green (color A).
2. Hold two strands of the blue yarn and one strand of the Blue Star blending filament together throughout the blue areas of the rug.
3. The river is worked in intarsia, so you'll need to use two balls of green yarn at one time. Twist the working yarns every time you change from one color to another by bringing the new color under and to the right of the old color.

■ PATTERN

CO 88 sts as follows: 36 sts in green, 19 sts in blue, and 33 sts with second ball of green.

Follow the chart.

Odd-numbered rows are the RS; even-numbered rows are the WS.

When chart is completed, BO all sts.

TIP

Remember to twist yarns between color changes.

FINISHING

Weave in ends.

Using a size H crochet hook and either metallic thread, slip stitch lines across the blue area of the rug to give the appearance of water ripples.

Suppliers

The following companies graciously supplied the beautiful yarns, materials, and equipment used in this book.

Bee Line Art Tools
makers of Bee Line Fabric Cutter
www.beelinearttools.com

Cascade Yarns
www.cascadeyarns.com

Coats and Clark
www.coatsandclark.com

Let Nola Do It
www.nolahooks.com
(314) 966-1813

Red Heart Yarns
www.redheart.com

Yarn Weights

Standard Yarn Weight System

Categories of yarn, gauge ranges, and recommended needle and hook sizes

Yarn Weight Symbol & Category Names	0 Lace	1 Super Fine	2 Fine	3 Light	4 Medium	5 Bulky	6 Super Bulky
Type of Yarns in Category	Fingering 10 count crochet thread	Sock, Fingering, Baby	Sport, Baby	DK, Light Worsted	Worsted, Afghan, Aran	Chunky, Craft, Rug	Bulky, Roving
Knit Gauge Range* in Stockinette Stitch to 4 inches	33 –40** sts	27–32 sts	23–26 sts	21–24 sts	16–20 sts	12–15 sts	6–11 sts
Recommended Needle in Metric Size Range	1.5–2.25 mm	2.25–3.25 mm	3.25–3.75 mm	3.75–4.5 mm	4.5–5.5 mm	5.5–8 mm	8 mm and larger
Recommended Needle U.S. Size Range	000 to 1	1 to 3	3 to 5	5 to 7	7 to 9	9 to 11	11 and larger
Crochet Gauge* Ranges in Single Crochet to 4 inch	32-42 double crochets**	21–32 sts	16–20 sts	12–17 sts	11–14 sts	8–11 sts	5–9 sts
Recommended Hook in Metric Size Range	Steel*** 1.6–1.4mm Regular hook 2.25 mm	2.25–3.5 mm	3.5–4.5 mm	4.5–5.5 mm	5.5–6.5 mm	6.5–9 mm	9 mm and larger
Recommended Hook U.S. Size Range	Steel*** 6, 7, 8 Regular hook B–1	B–1 to E–4	E–4 to 7	7 to I–9	I–9 to K–10½	K–10½ to M–13	M–13 and larger

* GUIDELINES ONLY: The above reflect the most commonly used gauges and needle or hook sizes for specific yarn categories.

** Lace weight yarns are usually knitted or crocheted on larger needles and hooks to create lacy, openwork patterns. Accordingly, a gauge range is difficult to determine. Always follow the gauge stated in your pattern.

*** Steel crochet hooks are sized differently from regular hooks--the higher the number, the smaller the hook, which is the reverse of regular hook sizing.

This Standards & Guidelines booklet and downloadable symbol artwork are available at: **YarnStandards.com**

Abbreviations

The following abbreviations are used throughout this book. Special stitches only used in a single pattern are defined in the notes at the beginning of the pattern.

CC	contrasting color		rem	remaining
CO	cast on		rep	repeat
k	knit		rnd(s)	round(s)
k2tog	knit 2 together		RS	right side
kwise	knitwise		Sl	slip
M1	make 1		ssk	slip, slip, knit
p	purl		st(s)	stitch(es)
p2tog	purl 2 together		tog	together
pm	place marker		WS	wrong side
prev	previous		wyib	with yarn in back
psso	pass slipped stitch over		wyif	with yarn in front
pwise	purlwise		yo	yarn over

Visual Index

 **2**
Forest Floor

 **9**
Crazy Combination Rug

 **12**
Brick Wall Rug

 **15**
Paul Klee Color Play

 **18**
Seaside Freeform Rug

 **24**
Color Wheel Rug

 **26**
Turner Watercolor Welt Rug

 **29**
Hit-and-Miss Rug

 **31**
Mondrian Meets Intarsia

 **34**
Giant Cables

38
Knitted
Penny Rug

52
Wool
Gizzard Rug

40
Buttonhole
Rug

55
Feelin'
Groovy
T-Shirt Rug

42
Goin'
Round in
Circles

57
Mad About
Plaid

46
String
It Up Rug

60
Denim Fluff
Rug

48
Have
a Heart

64
Diagonal
Stripes Rug

50
Holey
T-Shirt
Rug

66
Picasso
Harlequin
Rug